ANGLAIS

A1 → A2

Join the Team 6e

Édition 2010

Workbook

Sous la direction de :

Hélène Adrian
IA-IPR
Académie de Versailles

Cyril Dowling
Professeur agrégé
Lycée Français de Barcelone
Conseiller pédagogique

Sylvain Kustyan
Professeur certifié
Collège Blaise Pascal, Mazingarbe (62)
Formateur associé – Académie de Lille

Sylvie Sandra
Professeur certifié
Collège Vauban, Maubeuge (59)
Formatrice associée – Académie de Lille

Nathan

Édition : Fanny Husson, Fanny Blanchard
Illustrations : Philippe Chauvet
Laurent Audouin (pp. 62-65-81), Philippe Gady (pp. 50-54-109),
Bruno Liance (p. 119), Sébastien Telleschi (pp. 42-87-102-118),
Maureen Wingrove (pp. 35-65-96-110).
Iconographie : Valérie Delchambre
Conception de la maquette : Anne-Danièle Naname
Couverture : Grégoire Bourdin
Mise en pages : Christine Chenot

 – ISBN 978 209 173816 1

Sommaire

Welcome 4

Show what you know 4
Nice to meet you! 6
School time 8

Part 1 School friends 10

Unit 1 Back to school 11
Quick Check 16
Unit 2 I love history 17
Quick Check 22
My words 23
Check your progress 24

Part 2 Home, sweet home 26

Unit 3 Come in! 27
Quick Check 32
Unit 4 A garden party 33
Quick Check 38
My words 39
Check your progress 40

Part 3 Let's take a tour 42

Unit 5 Welcome to the Tower of London! 43
Quick Check 48
Unit 6 A scary visit 49
Quick Check 54
My words 55
Check your progress 56

Part 4 Family fun 58

Unit 7 What a family! 59
Quick Check 64
Unit 8 A picnic in Canterbury 65
Quick Check 70
Unit 9 We had a great time! 71
Quick Check 76
My words 77
Check your progress 78

Part 5 Show time 80

Unit 10 Time to act 81
Quick Check 86
Unit 11 Get ready for the show 87
Quick Check 92
Unit 12 A great musical 93
Quick Check 98
My words 99
Check your progress 100

Part 6 Across the sea 102

Unit 13 Off to Ireland 103
Quick Check 108
Unit 14 The magic island 109
Quick Check 114
My words 115
Check your progress 116

Part 7 Challenges 118

Unit 15 Who's going to win? 119
Quick Check 124
Unit 16 A champion team! 125
Quick Check 130
My words 131
Check your progress 132

Mes fiches de compétences 134

Écouter 134
Lire 136
Parler en continu 138
Parler en interaction 140
Écrire 142

Les logos utilisés dans le Workbook

Écouter

Lire

Parler en continu

Parler en interaction

Écrire

CD ÉLÈVE PISTE 4 — Document enregistré sur le CD élève

CD CLASSE — Document enregistré sur le CD classe

→ Renvoi au manuel

Show what you know

→ Manuel p. 10-11

Challenge 1 Meet a new friend

CD CLASSE

Ton nouveau correspondant t'a laissé un message ; écoute-le et note les informations que tu as repérées en t'aidant des illustrations.

....

....

....

Challenge 2 Meet the family

CD CLASSE

Écoute attentivement et note les informations que tu as repérées pour décrire les quatre garçons.

	Nom	Description physique
Boy 1	....	He has got ....
Boy 2	....	....
Boy 3	....	....
Boy 4	....	....

Challenge 3 Get in touch

Tu viens de recevoir un e-mail de ton correspondant. Quelle réponse vas-tu lui faire ?

a Recopie son e-mail.

....

....

....

b Réponds-lui en te servant de ses phrases et en t'aidant des énoncés suivants :

I am…

I like…

I don't like…

I live in…

I have got…

From: ....

to: ....

Object: ....

....

....

....

....

Challenge 4 A great visit

a Lis le prospectus (manuel p. 11) que ton correspondant américain t'a envoyé et note en français les informations importantes.

- ....
- ....
- ....

b Ces personnes souhaitent visiter le lieu décrit dans le prospectus. Lis les phrases et dis si la visite sera possible puis justifie ta réponse.

	oui	non	Justifie ta réponse
Mr et Mrs Smith sont à San Diego un mardi à 10 h du matin.	☐	☐	....
Tony et Julia sont à San Diego. Ils ont 50 dollars sur eux.	☐	☐	....
John a 25 ans. Il est à San Diego. Il est 21 h 30. Il a 90 dollars sur lui.	☐	☐	....
Scott est à San Diego un lundi en décembre. Il a 75 dollars.	☐	☐	....
Peter, Mary et leurs deux enfants (13 et 15 ans) sont à San Diego. Ils ont 300 dollars sur eux. Il est 19 h.	☐	☐	....

Challenge 5 What's your favourite food?

Interroge un des tes camarades pour qu'il (elle) réponde aux questions du formulaire. Puis note ses réponses.

Name: ....

Age: ....

City: ....

Favourite food: ....

Challenge 6 Spot the differences

Regarde attentivement les deux dessins p. 11 de ton manuel et repère au moins 5 différences entre les deux. Fais cinq phrases pour les décrire.

- ....
- ....
- ....
- ....
- ....

Nice to meet you!

→ Manuel p. 12-13

Listen to Chad and say who you are

CD CLASSE

a **Listen to Chad and answer his question.** ....

e **Read the signs and complete the missing letters.**

U_ _ _ _D S_ _ _ _S of A_ _ _ _ _ _A

D_ I_ Y_ _ _ _ _ _F

U_ _ _ _ _ K_ _ _ _ _ _ _

I L_ _ _ Y_ _

Listen to Tom and say who you are

CD CLASSE

a **Listen to Tom and answer his question.**

....

c **Play Bingo**

Choose a grid and write your name on it. Then listen and circle the numbers you hear. Raise your hand and say "Bingo" when your grid is complete.

Name: .... **Name:** .... **Name:** ....

A

7	15	29
30	45	67
79	82	93

B

7	13	21
34	40	62
70	86	99

C

7	14	17
30	45	62
78	85	99

d **Write the numbers in letters.**

13 ....

26 ....

38 ....

49 ....

14 ....

50 ....

Listen to Mrs Monroe and say where you live

b **Listen and match names and nationalities.**

Bob	Scottish
Sarah	French
Matt	English
Brenda	Welsh
Alex	Irish
Fiona	American

Listen to Zoe and say what you like

a **Listen to Zoe and answer her question.**

....

b **Read the poem and colour the picture.**

Blue is the sea,
Green is the grass,
White are the clouds
As they slowly pass.

Black are the crows,
Brown are the trees,
Red are the sails
Of a ship in the breeze.

YOUR TASK : Play the spy game

Imagine a new identity and complete the form below with your spy name, age, nationality...

Name: ....

Age: .... Male ☐ Female ☐

Nationality: ....

City: ....

Country: ....

Telephone number: ....

E-mail: ....

School time

→ Manuel p. 14-15

Have you got your book?

CD CLASSE

b Listen to Tom. What has he got in his school bag?
Tick the things Tom has got in his school bag.

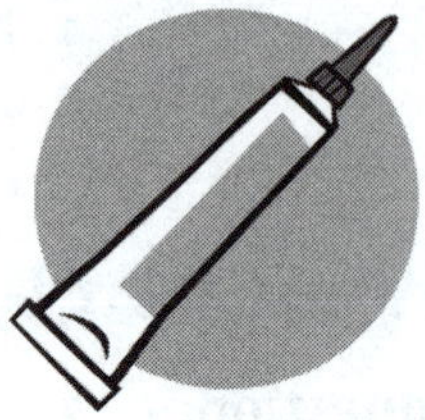

☐ ☐ ☐ ☐ ☐

c And what have you got in your school bag today?

....

....

....

Listen to your teacher!

CD CLASSE

b Listen and repeat. Then find the verb and write the missing letters.

O _ _ n!	W _ _ _ e!	A _ _ and a _ _ _ _ r!	L _ _ _ _ n!

What's the day, today?

CD CLASSE

a Listen and complete the poem. Then answer the question.

Every .... has 7 ....,
See how many you can say.
...................................., ..., ...,
...................................., ..., ...,
.... What's ....?
Today is ....

c **Find six months of the year in the grid.**

B	L	V	I	U	D	S	V	J	Y
R	E	B	M	E	C	E	D	Y	R
D	L	V	M	Z	V	P	G	F	A
Q	U	U	H	A	N	T	Y	D	U
M	A	R	C	H	Y	E	D	P	N
F	Y	D	S	A	O	M	L	H	A
R	N	O	V	E	M	B	E	R	J
J	U	L	Y	P	T	E	Q	F	M
X	C	J	N	G	S	R	X	E	Y
Z	A	G	S	B	F	W	M	X	F

DECEMBER

....

....

....

....

....

....

What time is it?

CD CLASSE

a **Listen and complete the clocks.**

b

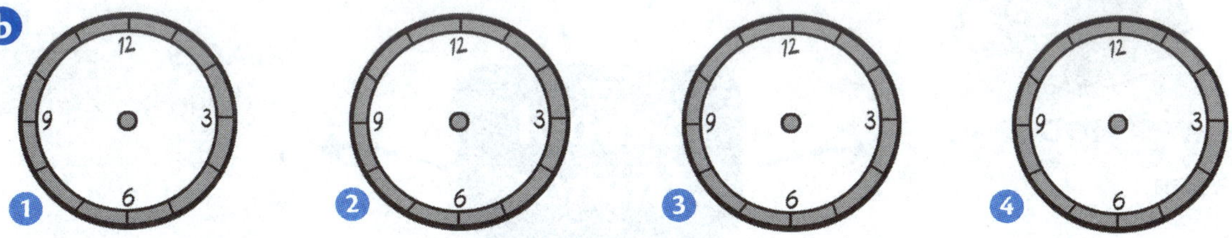

YOUR TASK : Pretend you are the teacher

2 **Do the registration: ask who is missing and complete the form.**

Teacher's name .... Class number ....

Date .... Time ....

List of missing pupils

- ill: ....
- late: ....
- other: ....

Signature ....

Part 1 School friends

Build up and organize your vocabulary

PEOPLE
- a pupil
- ....
- ....
- ....
- ....
- ....

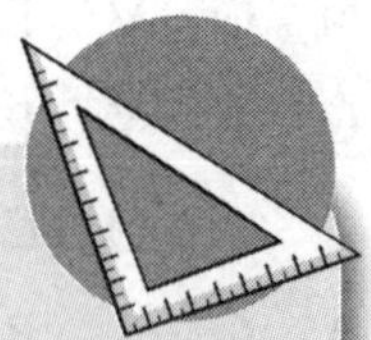

SUBJECTS
- Maths
- ....
- ....
- ....
- ....
- ....
- ....

IN MY SCHOOL BAG
- a pen
- ....
- ....
- ....
- ....
- ....

School friends

PLACES
- a school
- ....
- ....
- ....
- ....

EMOTIONS
- happy
- ....
- ....
- ....
- ....

ACTIONS
- write
- ....
- ....
- ....
- ....

Part 1 Unit 1 Back to school

Discover

→ Manuel p. 18

Wordgym

a Listen and repeat.

b Listen and write the subject.

....

....

2 Listen to John and take notes.

information	first friend	second friend
• Name	....	....
•	....	....
•	....	....
•	....	....

3 Listen to the voices and find out who is speaking.

	How many voices?	Male, female?	Age?	Name?	Other information
1	....	....	....	....	....
2	....	....	....	....	....
3	....	....	....	....	....
4	....	....	....	....	....

Listen and speak

CD ÉLÈVE PISTE 2 → Manuel p. 19

4 **a** **Look at the first picture: Who can you see?**

....

b **Listen to the beginning of the conversation: Where are they?**

My tactics

Quels sont les indices sonores qui te permettent de trouver où se passe la scène ?

....

....

....

c **Listen to the dialogue:**

Who can you hear? Who are they?

My tactics

Pour repérer qui parle, concentre-toi sur les voix et compte combien de personnes parlent.

....

How many...	Name?	Male or female?		Other information? (job...)
adults?	....	☐	☐	....
	....	☐	☐	....
young people?	....	☐	☐	....
	....	☐	☐	....
	....	☐	☐	....

d Listen and concentrate on Chad's reactions.

Chad is ....

Why? ....

....

Why? ....

....

Why? ....

e Write a sentence about each character.

- Mrs Monroe ....
- ....
- ....
- ....
- ....

Store up **Note 3 nouvelles expressions que tu as apprises dans la conversation.**

1. .... **2.** .... **3.** ....

Grammar Memo

Recopie le verbe de chaque phrase et retrouve la forme pleine.

1. *I'm happy.* .... → ....

2. *You're in my class.* .... → ....

3. *She's Australian.* .... → ....

4. *We're eleven.* .... → ....

Use what you know

→ Manuel p. 20

6 Write a few lines

You have received an e-mail from your English penfriend. Write an answer.

From: ....

to: migel-kennedy@yahoo.com.uk

Object: ....

....

....

....

....

HAVE FUN

CD CLASSE

Happy to go back to school

Complete the song:

.... happy, ... happy to go to school.
.... happy, ... happy to go to school.
.... happy, ... happy to go to school.
Oh! .... happy to go back to school.

My name .... Jake and ....!
His name .... Ben, her name .... Molly!
Good morning, miss! Hello, sir!
.... to go back to school.

7 YOUR TASK

Make a quiz about your school. Write down your questions and your classmates' answers.

	Questions	Answers	
		Classmate 1:	Classmate 2: ....
1	......................................?	....	....
2	......................................?	....	....
3	......................................?	....	....
4	......................................?	....	....
5	......................................?	....	....

Homework

Exercice 1

Remets ces questions dans l'ordre. N'oublie pas la ponctuation. Puis imagine une réponse.

1. old / is / how / Maggie

....

Maybe ....

2. name / what / is / his

....

I think ....

3. she / is / from / where

....

Maybe ....

4. is / boy / who / that

....

I think ....

5. Paul / where / Peter / are / and

....

I think ....

Exercice 2

Présente ces deux nouveaux élèves. Rédige des phrases complètes et évite les répétitions.

1. ....

....

2. ....

....

Exercice 3

Malcolm n'est pas très bon en histoire-géographie. Corrige ses erreurs.

1. Manchester is the capital city of the United Kingdom. Manchester ....
.... It's ....
2. Prince Harry and Prince William are American.

....

3. Big Ben is in Paris. ....
4. Ireland is a big city. ....
5. Glasgow and Edinburgh are in Wales.

....

Quick check

CD CLASSE

→ Manuel p. 19

1 **Écoute et note qui parle.**

Nombre de voix : .... Voix féminines : .... Voix masculines : ....

Noms : ....

☐ **Je sais repérer des voix.**

2 **Écoute et complète le tableau.**

Name	Dane	Marsha
....	....	....
....	....	....
....	....	....

☐ **Je sais comprendre des informations sur l'identité de quelqu'un.**

3 **Lis un passage du journal intime de Lily et dis si ces affirmations sont vraies ou fausses. Justifie ta réponse.**

Dear Diary,
I'm so happy to go back to school. A new pupil is in my class. His name is Chris. He's very special. I think he's Canadian because he's very tall and strong. I know he's eleven, just like me and...

	vrai	faux	justifie ta réponse
1. Chris est dans la classe de Lily.	☐	☐	....
2. Chris a 11 ans.	☐	☐	....
3. Lily pense que Chris est canadien.	☐	☐	....
4. Lily n'est pas contente de retourner à l'école.	☐	☐	....

☐ **Je sais reconnaître si des informations sont correctes.**

4 **Pose 4 questions à ton meilleur ami sur son chanteur préféré.**

1. Name: ....?

2. Age: ....?

3. Nationality: ....?

4. Origin: ....?

☐ **Je sais me renseigner sur l'identité de quelqu'un.**

Part 1

Unit 2 I love history

Discover

→ Manuel p. 24

Wordgym

Choose the words corresponding to the pictures and write them down.

open the door | go to the board | turn on the light | draw

close the window | write the date | read | take off my jacket

1. ....

2. ....

3. ....

4. ....

5. ....

6. ....

7. ....

8. ....

2 Listen again and complete the questions.

1. Miss, can .... put my paper in the bin?
2. I don't understand. .... explain?
3. I can't hear you. .... repeat, please?
4. I can't see. .... move to one side, please?

Listen and speak

CD ÉLÈVE PISTE 3 → Manuel p. 25

4 **a** **Look at the first picture. Who can you see? Guess what the subject of the class is.**

Names: ……………………………………………………………………

Subject of the class: ……………………………………………………………

• **Then listen to the conversation and check your answers.**

……………………………………………………………………………………

……………………………………………………………………………………

My tactics

Quels mots as-tu repérés pour déterminer la matière que les élèves étudient ?

……………………………………………………………………………………

b **Listen to the beginning of the conversation and focus on Scarlett and Mrs Preston. Tick the right answer. Speak with the class.**

	sorry	angry	nice	surprised
Scarlett	☐	☐	☐	☐
Mrs Preston	☐	☐	☐	☐

My tactics

Comment as-tu déduis les sentiments des personnages ?

……………………………………………………………………………………

……………………………………………………………………………………

• **Now recap:** Scarlett is …………………… because ……………………………

Mrs Preston is …………………… because she says ……………………………

c **Listen and focus on the lesson. What is the lesson about?**

☐ 

☐ 

☐ 

☐ Other: ……………………………………………………………………

My tactics

Quels mots as-tu repérés pour déterminer le thème de la leçon ?

....

d Listen again and focus on Mrs Preston's questions. Complete the information.

the question is about:	answer
•	....
•	....
•	....

e Listen again and focus on Tom's emotions.

- **Tick the right answer.**

 ☐  ☐  ☐

- **Now recap:** Tom is .... because ....

f Imagine a title for the story.

....

Store up your vocabulary

Note trois expressions pour montrer ton admiration :

1. .... **2.** .... **3.** ....

Que dis-tu pour excuser un retard ?

....

Grammar Memo

1 Observe bien les phrases suivantes :

a. *Mrs Preston:"Come in!"*

b. *Scarlett: "Can I come in, please?"*

2 Observe la ponctuation et dis de quel type de phrase il s'agit :

a. Une phrase .... C'est un ....

b. Une phrase .... C'est une ....

3 Explique maintenant comment tu construis :

a. un ordre : ....

b. une demande polie : ....

Use what you know

→ Manuel p. 26

5 Speak in pairs

a Listen to the TV game and take notes.

- Who can you hear? ....
- What is the topic of the game? ....
- Focus on the two questions: Who gives the right answer? ....

....

b Prepare your questions about London.

- Capital city of England: ....
- River : ....
- ....: ....
- ....: ....
- ....: ....

6 YOUR TASK

Be the club teacher: Your teacher asks you to start the club.
Write important words to prepare your speech.

INSTRUCTIONS

- Discipline ....
- Rules ....

....

- Equipment (clothes...) ....
- Activities ....

....

Homework

Exercice 1

Complète ces phrases :

a. Are you ready? ....'s start!

b. .... you .... me the name of the capital city of France?

c. Hmm… I .... it – Paris!

d. Congratulations! ....'s continue ! .... you .... me the name of the city where Big Ben is?

e. I .... it's in London.

Exercice 2

Complète les phrases avec les mots suivants pour qu'elles gardent le même sens.

happy angry easy finish great

a. Scarlett is fabulous. = she's ....

b. It's not difficult. = it's ....

c. Let's stop the game. = let's ....

d. Scarlett isn't sad. = she's ....

e. Mrs Preston is cross. = she's ....

Exercice 3

Retrouve les quatre questions posées par ces personnes.

1. ....

2. ....

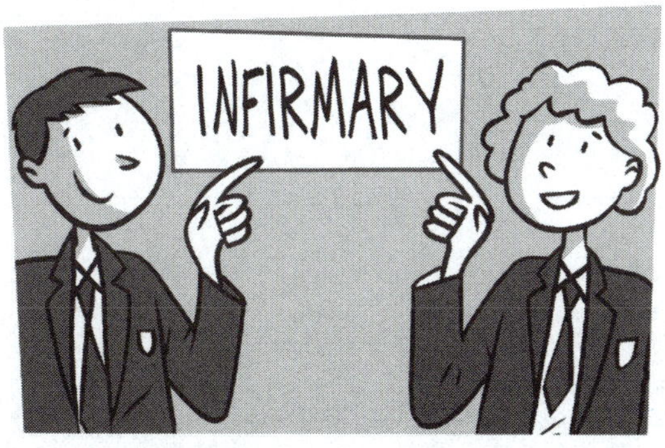

3. ....

4. ....

Quick check

→ Manuel p. 25

1 **Écoute ces différentes personnes. Quels sentiments expriment-elles ?**

a. ....

b. ....

c. ....

d. ....

e. ....

☐ **Je sais déterminer un sentiment à partir d'une intonation.**

2 **Tu dois réagir en classe aux 5 situations suivantes. Écris les questions que tu poserais quand...**

1. ... tu as froid : ....

2. ... tu veux aider un camarade : ....

3. ... tu ne vois pas bien parce qu'il fait presque nuit : ....

....

4. ... tu ne te sens pas bien : ....

5. ... tu veux aller au tableau : ....

☐ **Je sais demander la permission.**

3 **Écris un e-mail pour demander des renseignements à ton correspondant : numéro de téléphone, photo, ville, réponse rapide.**

From: ....

to: ....

Object: ....

....

....

....

....

....

....

....

....

☐ **Je sais écrire un e-mail pour demander des renseignements.**

Part 1

My words

Les verbes

close : fermer
come in : entrer
draw : dessiner
forget : oublier
give : donner
go to : aller à
listen to : écouter
look at : regarder
open : ouvrir
read : lire
remember : se souvenir
repeat : répéter
see : voir
sing : chanter
sleep : dormir
speak : parler
talk : parler
take : prendre

Les adjectifs

angry : en colère
American : américain(e)
Australian : australien(enne)
difficult : difficile
easy : facile
English : anglais(e)
excited : enjoué, enthousiaste
happy : heureux(euse)
incredible : incroyable
late : en retard
new : nouveau
nice : sympathique
sad : triste
Scottish : écossais
sorry : désolé(e)

Les noms

Art : les arts plastiques
Biology : la biologie
a cafeteria : une cantine
a classroom : une salle de classe
a headmaster : un principal
Geography : la géographie
History : l'histoire
a king : un roi
Maths : les mathématiques
a playground : une cour de récréation
PE : l'E.P.S.
a pupil : un(e) élève
a queen : une reine
a subject : une matière
a teacher : un professeur
a uniform : un uniforme
year 7 : la classe de 6e

Les mots interrogatifs

Who? : qui ?
Where? : où ?
What? : que, quel ?
Why? : pourquoi ?

Expressions à retenir

Congratulations! : Félicitations !
That's alright! That's ok! : C'est bon!

Maintenant je connais :

	☹	😐	☺
→ des expressions pour présenter quelqu'un et parler de ses sentiments	☐	☐	☐
→ des phrases pour demander quelque chose	☐	☐	☐
→ le lexique de l'école	☐	☐	☐

Part 1 Check your progress

1 LISTEN

→ Manuel p. 29

Stop chatting!

J'ai su :

A1

- ☐ **1.** dire qui parle et où se passe la scène.

....

....

....

- ☐ **2.** dire ce que cette personne demande.

....

....

....

....

A1+

- ☐ **3.** repérer ses sentiments à la fin de la conversation.

....

2 READ

→ Manuel p. 29

Can you help me?

J'ai su :

A1

- ☐ **1.** dire ce qu'il / elle demande.

....

....

....

A1+

- ☐ **2.** repérer qui a envoyé l'e-mail et dire sa nationalité.

....

- ☐ **3.** repérer qui est le destinataire et dire sa nationalité.

....

3 SPEAK

→ Manuel p. 29

Pupils at Hogwarts

J'ai su :

A1 ☐ **1.** donner des informations sur leur identité : nom, âge, nationalité, pays d'origine.

A1+ ☐ **2.** expliquer pourquoi je les apprécie.

4 WRITE

→ Manuel p. 29

English class rules

J'ai su :

A1 ☐ **1.** noter 3 choses que je dois faire.

A1+ ☐ **2.** noter 3 choses que je ne dois pas faire.

☐ **3.** faire une affiche (titre, couleurs, illustrations, mise en page).

English class rules

Part 2

Home, sweet home

Build up and organize your vocabulary

OUTSIDE
- a garden
- ....
- ....
- ....
- ....
- ....

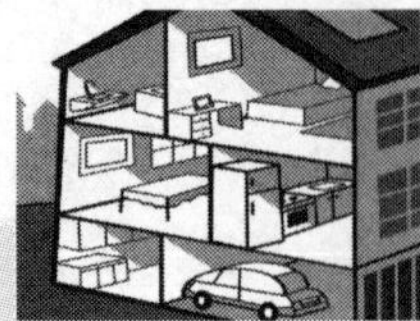

INSIDE
- a bedroom
- ....
- ....
- ....
- ....
- ....
- ....

BEDROOM
- a bed
- ....
- ....
- ....
- ....
- ....
- ....

A HOUSE

Home, sweet home

FOOD
- ....
- ....
- ....
- ....
- ....
- ....
- ....

FAMILY
- a father
- ....
- ....
- ....
- ....
- ....
- ....

DRINKS
- ....
- ....
- ....
- ....
- ....

PETS
- a dog
- ....
- ....
- ....
- ....

Part 2

Unit 3 Come in!

Discover

→ Manuel p. 34

Wordgym

a Look at picture 1 and write the word corresponding to the number.

bed **a desk** **toys** **a cupboard** **a lamp** **shelves**

Ex.: bed is n°1

1

2

① .... ② .... ③ ....

④ .... ⑤ .... ⑥ ....

b Look at pictures 1 and 2 and spot the four differences.

- ....
- ....
- ....
- ....

3 Listen and say where the people are. CD CLASSE

	Who? (man, woman, boy, girl...)	Where? (kitchen, bedroom...)	Clues (sounds, words...)
a			
b			
c			
d			

Listen and speak

CD ÉLÈVE PISTE 5

→ Manuel p. 35

4 **a** **Look at the first picture in your book p. 35 and imagine where the boys are.**

My tactics

Note ici ce qui te permet de déterminer chez qui la scène se passe.

....

....

At Chad's ☐ At Tom's ☐ At Scarlett's ☐

b **Now listen and check your answer.**

They are at .... because .... says ....

....

c **Listen and visit the house with the boys.**

My tactics

Écoute bien les bruits. Ils t'aideront à déterminer où se trouvent les personnages.
Prends des notes pendant l'écoute.

Indice sonore	Pièce
....	....
....	....
....	....

Now say where they are:

First, Chad and Tom are ...., then they ....
and finally ....

d **Listen and find information about Chad and Tom's families. Complete with "Yes", "No", "I don't know".**

	Chad	Tom
sister	....	....
brother	....	....

e **Listen again and find information about Zoe.**

- Her things: ....
- Her pets: ....

f **Listen and tick Tom's things.**

 ☐
 ☐
 ☐
 ☐
 ☐
 ☐
 ☐
 ☐
 ☐
 ☐

g **Listen again and recap. Give lots of details about Tom.**

....

....

....

h **Listen and focus on Chad's reactions. Tick the right answer and justify.**

☐ I think he likes Tom's house. ☐ I think he doesn't like Tom's house.

because he says ....

Store up your vocabulary

Note 2 nouvelles expressions que tu as apprises dans la conversation.

1

1. You ....
2. My room ....

2

Grammar Memo

Observe les phrases suivantes :

1. *You've got a lot of DVDs.*
2. *Have you got a TV in your room?*
3. *You haven't got a little sister.*

- Quel est le point commun entre ces trois phrases ?

Elles sont construites avec .... et elles expriment la ....

Use what you know

→ Manuel p. 36

5 Speak in pairs

Ask your classmate questions about the things in his/her bedroom. Complete the grid with his/her answers.

	How many?	Where?
Furniture	....	....
Electronics	....	....
Other things	....	....

6 YOUR TASK

Write a short note for the school magazine about your favourite star's bedroom.

2 Prepare your note: List what he/she's got in his/her bedroom and give details.

Star:		
	How many?	Where?
Furniture	....	....
Electronics	....	....
Other things	....	....

4 Write your note.

....

....

....

Homework

Exercice 1

Regarde la « check list » de Chad et récapitule ce qu'il a et ce qu'il n'a pas dans son sac.

1. ....
2. ....
3. ....
4. ....
5. ....

Exercice 2

Tu viens de te faire un nouvel ami.
Pose-lui 4 questions sur ce qu'il a dans sa chambre.

1. Posters: .... ?
2. Beds: .... ?
3. Dvds: .... ?
4. ....: .... ?

Exercice 3

Écris un e-mail à ton correspondant afin de lui décrire ta chambre.

From: ....

to: steve_Moore@hotmail.com

Object: My bedroom

....

....

....

....

....

Quick check

CD CLASSE → Manuel p. 35

1 **Écoute et note qui parle et où se trouvent ces personnes.**

Qui ?	Où ?
....	....
....	....
....	....
....	....

☐ **Je sais repérer qui parle et où se passe la scène.**

2 **Écoute et complète le tableau.**

	Tom	Marsha
books	....	....
....	....	....
....	....	....

☐ **Je sais repérer ce que quelqu'un possède ou pas.**

3 **Écoute et dis si ces affirmations sont vraies ou fausses.**
Justifie ta réponse en français.

	vrai	faux
1. Martha a des animaux domestiques dans sa chambre.	☐	☐
2. Sa sœur n'a pas de chien mais elle a un chat.	☐	☐
3. Martha n'a pas d'ordinateur dans sa chambre.	☐	☐
4. Son lit est à côté de son armoire.	☐	☐

☐ **Je sais repérer les objets et les localiser dans l'espace.**

4 **Prépare 4 questions que tu poseras à l'assitant(e) anglais(e) de ton collège sur les thèmes suivants :** *identity , family, pets, objects.*

....

....

....

....

☐ **Je sais questionner quelqu'un sur ce qu'il / elle possède.**

Unit 4 A garden party

Discover

Manuel p. 40

Wordgym

Create a breakfast menu, a lunch menu and a dinner menu.

Use: chicken | ice cream | cake | salad | vegetables | water | milk | cereal | chips | fruit | orange juice | sausages | baked beans | toast

Breakfast
* ....
* ....
* ....
* ....
* ....
* ....

Lunch menu
....
....
....
....
....
....
....
....
....

Dinner
o ....
o ....
o ....
o ....
o ....
o ....
o ....
o ....
o ....

2 Listen to the interview and fill in the grid. Say what the boy likes and doesn't like.

CD CLASSE

Name	🙂	☹
....	....	....

Listen and speak

CD ÉLÈVE PISTE 6

→ Manuel p. 41

4 **a** **Look at the first picture in your book. Who can you see? Where are the characters?**

- Names: ....
- Place: ....

Then listen to the beginning of the conversation and check your ideas.

....

....

My tactics

Quels mots te permettent de vérifier tes réponses ?

....

....

b **Listen and focus on Tom and Chad's reactions. Say how they feel.**

- **Tick the right pictures.**

☐ angry ☐ surprised ☐ happy ☐ sad

- **Then speak with the class and present the situation.**

....

....

c **Listen again and focus on Chad's comments at the barbecue. Write the words you hear.**

....

....

....

d Listen and focus on Scarlett and her family. Complete the information.

- First name: ....
- Last name: ....
- Nationality: ....
- Country and town where she lives: ....
- Country and town where her mother lives: ....
- Country and town where her father lives: ....

e Listen again and focus on Chad. Complete the information.

- His plate: ....
- His hobbies (sports): ....

....

f Listen to the end of the story and choose the right picture.

☐

☐

g Imagine a title for the story.

....

Store up your vocabulary

Note trois onomatopées que tu as entendues dans la conversation.

1. ....

2. ....

3. ....

Grammar Memo

1 Observe les phrases suivantes :

a. *I **love** barbecues.*
b. *My father **works** in New York.*
c. *Scarlett and her mum **live** in England.*

Les verbes ne se conjuguent pas lorsqu'ils sont au présent simple sauf à la ………… personne du ………………………… où on ajoute un ………… à la base verbale.

2 Observe les phrases suivantes à la forme interrogative et à la forme négative.

a. ***Do** you like chicken?*
b. *They **don't** work here.*
c. ***Does** he live in England?*
d. *He **doesn't** live in England.*

À la forme interrogative, on emploie l'auxiliaire ………………………… ou ………………………… : il se place devant …………………………

À la forme négative, il devient ………………………… ou ………………………… et se place devant …………………………

Use what you know

→ Manuel p. 42

6 Speak in pairs

Interview a classmate (identity, likes and dislikes, hobbies) and write down his/her answers.

First name: ……………………………………………… Last name: ………………………………………………

Food	☺	☹
………………………………		
………………………………		
………………………………		
………………………………		
………………………………		

Hobbies	☺	☹
………………………………		
………………………………		
………………………………		

Homework

Exercice 1

Complète les phrases suivantes avec le verbe « *like* » au présent simple à la forme qui convient.

a. Peter .... tennis. He's very good at it.

b. Steve .... meat. He thinks it's cruel to eat animals!

c. Yummy! I .... ice cream a lot. I think it's delicious.

d. Lucy .... French. She thinks it's too difficult.

e. Yuck! I .... beer! I think it's disgusting!

Exercice 2

Voici l'emploi du temps de ton club de sport. Tu décris à ta grand-mère les sports que tu fais cette année.

Monday	Tuesday	Wednesday	Thursday	Friday	Saturday
			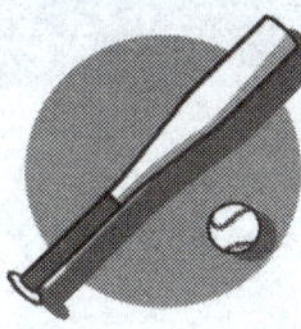		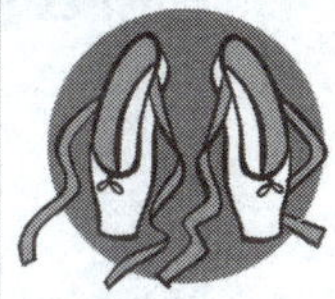

« This year, on ...., I ....

....

....

.... »

Exercice 3

Complète le dialogue ci-dessous.

Steve: Do you .... milk?

Lucy: Yes, I .... And what about you?

Steve: No, ..., but I .... ice cream very much!

Lucy: ....?

Steve: Yes, I do. I play tennis on Tuesdays. ....?

Lucy: No I don't. I think rugby is too dangerous.

Steve: .... your brother ....?

Lucy: Yes, he does! My brother is very good at basket ball! He .... on Fridays.

Quick check

CD CLASSE → Manuel p. 41

1 Écoute ces différentes personnes. Note les onomatopées qu'elles utilisent, et déduis-en leurs sentiments.

a. ....
b. ....
c. ....
d. ....
e. ....

☐ **Je sais associer une onomatopée à un sentiment.**

2 Voici les réponses de M. Carter à une enquête de magazine. Utilise-les pour rédiger un court paragraphe.

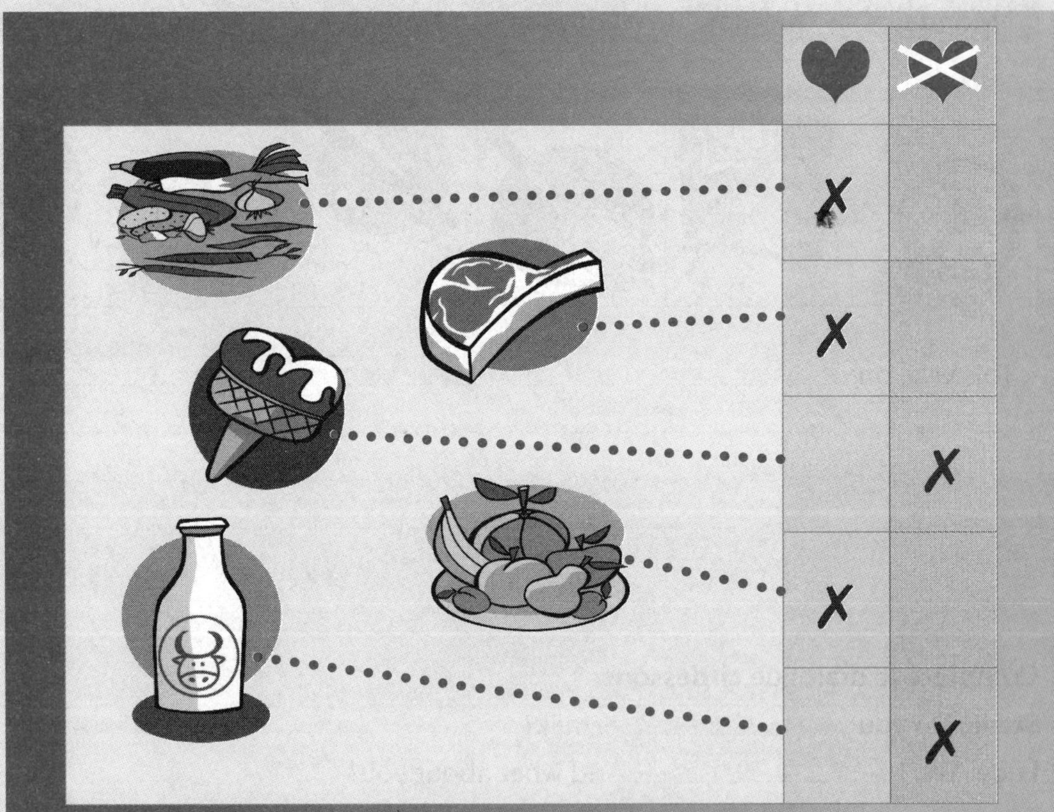

Mr Carter ....
....
....
....

☐ **Je sais parler des goûts de quelqu'un.**

Part 2

My words

Les verbes

drink : boire
eat : manger
like : aimer
live : vivre
play : jouer
work : travailler

Les adjectifs

angry : en colère
happy : content(e)
hungry : qui a faim
sad : triste
sorry : désolé(e)
thirsty : qui a soif

Les noms

• The house

a bathroom : une salle de bain
a bed : un lit
a bedroom : une chambre
a computer : un ordinateur
a cupboard : un placard
a desk : un bureau
a door : une porte
a garden : le jardin
a kitchen : une cuisine
a living-room : un salon
a party : une fête
a shelf (pluriel : shelves) : une étagère
a wall : un mur
a window : une fenêtre

• Pets

a cat : un chat
a dog : un chien
a fish (pluriel : fish) : un poisson
a hamster : un hamster
a mouse (pluriel : mice) : une souris

• Food

chicken : du poulet
chips : des frites
fruit : des fruits
milk : du lait
orange juice : du jus d'orange
vegetables : des légumes
water : de l'eau

Les prépositions

downstairs : en bas
in : dans
near : près de
next to : à côté
on : sur
under : en dessous
upstairs : en haut (à l'étage)

Les onomatopées

ouch! : aïe ! **pooh! :** pfff ! **shh! :** chut !
yuck! : beurk ! **yummy! :** miam-miam !

Maintenant je connais du vocabulaire pour :

	☹	😐	☺
→ présenter ma maison	☐	☐	☐
→ parler de mes goûts	☐	☐	☐
→ exprimer mes sentiments	☐	☐	☐

Part 2 Check your progress

1 LISTEN

→ Manuel p. 45

My house, my life

J'ai su :

A1
- ☐ **1.** relever des informations concernant l'identité de cet adolescent, ses goûts.

A1+
- ☐ **2.** comprendre la description de sa maison et de sa chambre.
- ☐ **3.** commenter la réaction de ses parents.

2 READ

→ Manuel p. 45

My grandma

J'ai su :

A1
- ☐ 1. repérer de qui elle parle dans son texte.
- ☐ 2. décrire la maison de cette personne.

A1+
- ☐ 3. décrire ses goûts et ses activités.
- ☐ 4. expliquer la dernière phrase du texte.

3 SPEAK

→ Manuel p. 45

My favourite pet

J'ai su :

A1 ☐ 1. présenter mon animal domestique préféré (identité, lieu de vie, goûts).

....

....

....

A1+ ☐ 2. dire quels sont ses endroits préférés dans la maison, dans ma chambre, quand je joue avec lui.

....

....

4 WRITE

→ Manuel p. 45

My new friend!

J'ai su :

A1 ☐ 1. présenter mon ami(e) (identité).

....

A1+ ☐ 2. parler de sa famille (parents, frères et sœurs).

....

☐ 3. décrire sa maison et sa chambre.

....

☐ 4. parler de ses goûts.

....

Part 3 Let's take a tour

Build up and organize your vocabulary

Let's take a tour

MEANS OF TRANSPORT
- a bus
- ....
- ....
- ....
- ....

ON A MAP
- a street
- ....
- ....
- ....
- ....
- ....

LONDON MONUMENTS
- The British Museum
- ....
- ....
- ....
- ....
- ....

PREPOSITIONS
- on
- ....
- ....
- ....
- ....
- ....

MORE WORDS
- ....
- ....
- ....
- ....

DIRECTIONS
- turn right
- ....
- ....
- ....

Part 3

Unit 5 Welcome to the Tower of London!

Discover

→ Manuel p. 50

1 **Listen to the poem and draw the spiders.**

Wordgym

a **Write the prepositions corresponding to the following drawings.**

b **Listen to the description of a haunted manor and draw the elements you hear.**

Read and speak

→ Manuel p. 51

4 Look at the document in your book p. 51 and say what sort of document it is.

☐ a tourist brochure ☐ a horror film poster ☐ a book about London

a What is there to see in this castle?
Read the document and make a list.

....

....

My tactics

Note les mots transparents qui t'ont aidé à comprendre l'ensemble du document.

....

....

....

....

b These people want to visit the Tower of London. Say if it is possible or not.
Explain why.

	yes	no
• Mr. Clark is in London. It is Monday afternoon; it's 5 p.m.	☐	☐

....

....

	yes	no
• Lucy is in London. She's got £3 (pounds).	☐	☐

....

....

	yes	no
• It's Wednesday afternoon. It's 2 p.m. Mr. Jones is in Oxford.	☐	☐

....

....

c Say if these people would like the Tower of London or not.

	yes	no
• Mr. Higgins is a history teacher. He loves stories of kings and queens.	☐	☐
• Peter is 13 years old. He only likes sports and video games! He doesn't like history.	☐	☐
• Julia is 8 years old. She is scared of everything!	☐	☐

d Make a list of what you prefer at the Tower of London.

- .... • ....
- .... • ....

Now explain why it's an interesting monument.

....

....

e Look at the document again and find three other interesting places to visit in London.

....

....

....

f Quiz your friends about the Tower of London. Prepare three questions and write down the answers.

Ex.: *Is there a restaurant at the Tower of London?*
No, there isn't!

- **Questions**

....

....

....

- **Answers**

....

....

....

Grammar Memo

Pour dire « il y a » en anglais :

- j'utilise .... suivi d'un nom au singulier.
- j'utilise .... suivi d'un nom au pluriel.

Use what you know

→ Manuel p. 52

6 Write a few lines

Write a postcard to your friend about your visit to the Tower of London. Explain why the Tower of London is an interesting monument.

7 YOUR TASK

Buying souvenirs in a shop.
Listen to the conversation and fill in the blanks. CD CLASSE

Shopkeeper: Good .... Sir, Good .... Madam.

Customer: ....!

Shopkeeper: How can I .... you?

Customer: Well, we .... to buy souvenirs. .... is this mug?

Shopkeeper: .... £6.50.

Customer: Ok, two mugs ....

Shopkeeper: Two mugs. Ok (*wrapping*). That's £13 Madam. Here you are.

Customer: Thank you.

Shopkeeper: You're ....

Customer: ....

Store up your vocabulary

Note les expressions utiles que tu as apprises dans la conversation.

1. G..! 2. How ....?
3. How ....?
4. T....................................! You ....
5. You're .... B........... B...........!

Homework

Exercice 1

Complète les phrases suivantes avec « *there is* » ou « *there are* ». Puis traduis-les en français.

1. .... a lot of black spiders in this room.

....

2. .... a big raven at the door.

....

3. .... a beautiful sword next to the fireplace.

....

4. .... famous castles in London?

....

5. .... large parks in London?

....

Exercice 2

À l'aide du document p. 51 de ton manuel, dis si les affirmations suivantes sont vraies ou fausses. Corrige les phrases si nécessaire.

	vrai	faux
1. At the Tower of London, there are eight ravens.	☐	☐
....		
2. There is the Imperial State Crown.	☐	☐
....		
3. There are a lot of ghosts at the Tower of London.	☐	☐
....		
4. There are no guards at the Tower of London.	☐	☐
....		
5. The Tower of London is open on Monday at 8 a.m.	☐	☐
....		

Exercice 3

Regarde le dessin et retrouve les noms des objets qui correspondent aux indices suivants :

1. It's next to the chair: ....
2. It's under the table: ....
3. It's behind the door: ....
4. It's between the table and the fireplace:

....

5. It's in the clock: ....

Quick check

→ Manuel p. 51

1 **Lis la brochure et écris en quelques lignes en anglais les informations que tu as comprises.**

☐ Je sais comprendre les informations essentielles d'une brochure touristique.

2 **a Écoute attentivement et complète le dessin ci-dessous.**

b Écoute et associe le nom des personnages au dessin qui correspond.

☐ Je peux situer des animaux et des personnes dans l'espace.

Unit 6 A scary visit

Discover

→ Manuel p. 56

1 **Listen and draw the itinerary.** CD CLASSE

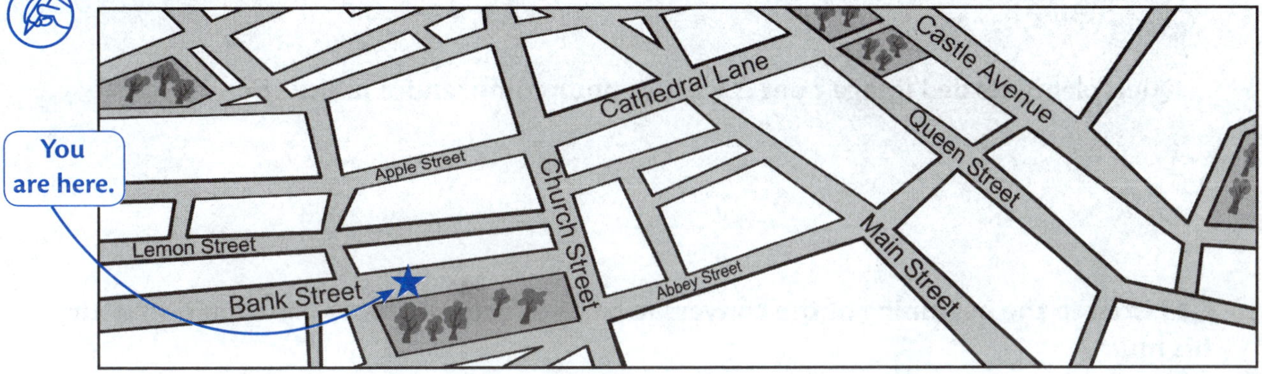

Wordgym

Complete the drawing with the words below.

hair ear eye nose mouth tooth neck shoulder
arm hand finger stomach leg knee foot toe

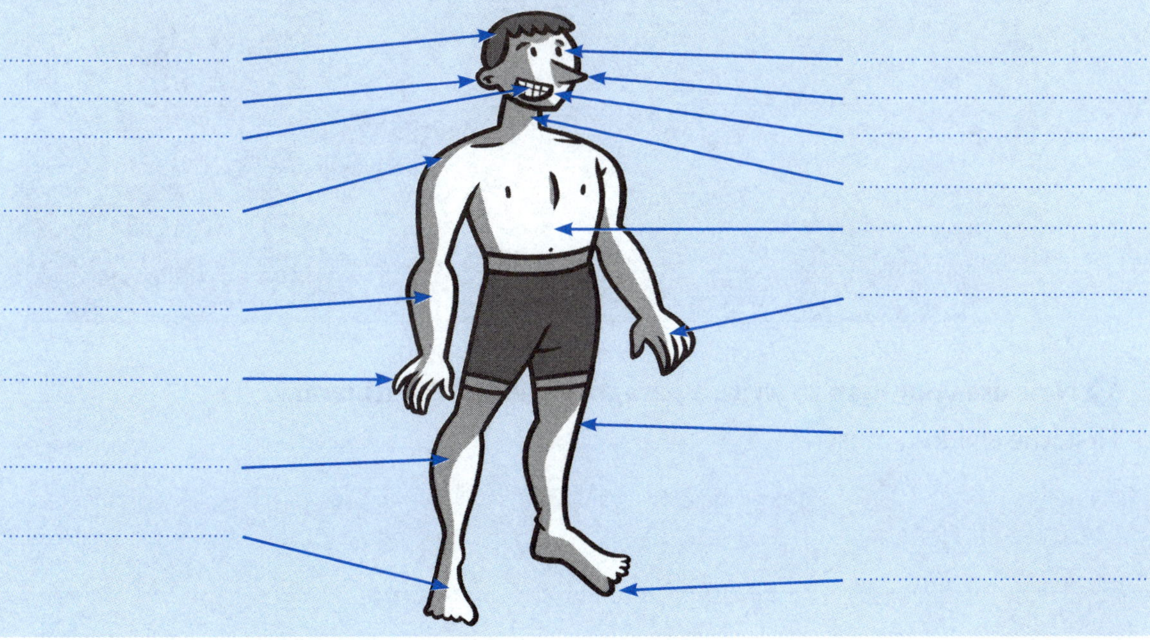

Listen and speak

CD ÉLÈVE PISTE 8 → Manuel p. 57

3 **a** **Look at the first picture in your book p. 57 and complete.**

- Names: ....
- Place: ....

☐ happy ☐ embarrassed ☐ angry

My tactics

Quels éléments de l'image t'ont été utiles pour comprendre la situation ?

....

....

b **Listen to the beginning of the conversation and focus on Tom's conversation with his mum.**

- Circle with a red pen the place where the characters are.
- Circle with a green pen the place where they want to go.
- Listen carefully and draw the itinerary with a blue pen.

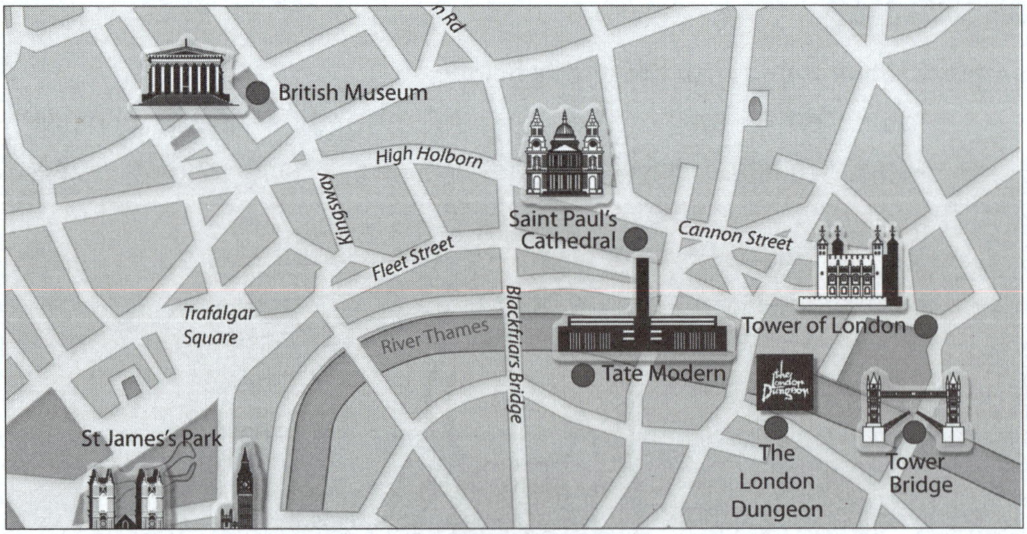

c **Now use your map to write a paragraph about the itinerary.**

First, the children must ....

....

....

....

....

d Look at the second picture. Where are they? Are they excited? Scared? Sad?

- Place: ....
- Feelings: ....

....

My tactics

Quels éléments de l'image as-tu utilisés pour situer la scène ?

....

....

e Listen and focus on the characters' feelings and reactions. Match the names with the drawings.

Chad • Tom • Zoe •

f Listen to the end of the conversation and find a title for the end of the conversation.

....

Store up your vocabulary

1. Note les adjectifs que tu connais pour exprimer des sentiments :

....

2. Note une expression pour dire ce que quelqu'un est capable de faire :

....

3. Note une expression pour dire ce que quelqu'un ne doit pas faire :

....

Grammar Memo

- Pour parler de ce que quelqu'un est capable ou n'est pas capable de faire, tu utilises l'auxiliaire : .... / ....
- Pour parler de ce que quelqu'un doit ou ne doit pas faire, tu utilises l'auxiliaire : .... / ....

Use what you know

→ Manuel p. 58

4 Speak for a minute

b Your best friend is absent. Write him an e-mail about the teacher's recommendations for the trip.

From: ....

to: ....

Object: ....

....

....

....

....

....

....

....

....

6 YOUR TASK

You're at the Tower of London and want to go to Buckingham Palace. You haven't got a map. You call your English friend who tells you the way.

Prepare your itinerary with the map of London in your book (p. 62). Write down the names of the streets:

1. ....

2. ....

3. ....

4. ....

5. ....

Homework

Exercice 1

Complète les phrases suivantes avec *can* ou *can't*. Traduis-les ensuite en français.

1. I am very athletic! I .... play football and basket ball; I .... swim very well. But I .... ride a horse.

....

....

2. Ghosts .... fly, but I really think they .... run! They have got no legs! ....

....

3. .... you see the ravens next to Wakefield Tower? Don't worry, they .... fly! ....

....

4. My sister .... run very fast because she is a little girl.

....

Exercice 2

Regarde le plan et donne les instructions nécessaires pour aller du *White Horse Hotel* au *Magic Cinema Complex*.

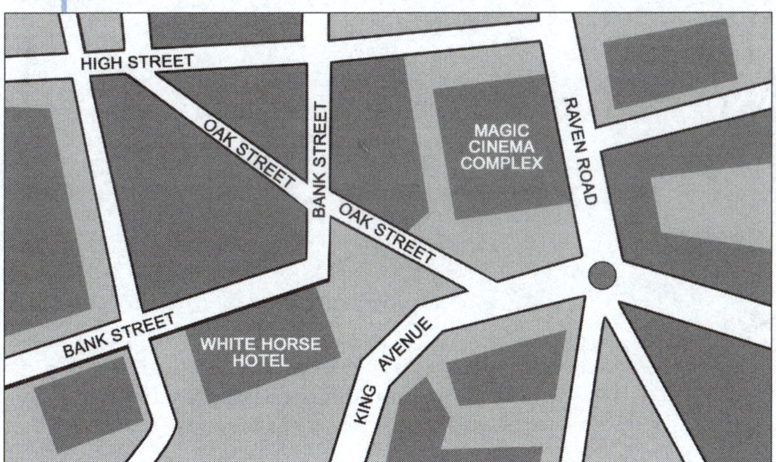

....

....

....

....

....

....

....

....

....

....

....

....

Exercice 3

Regarde les panneaux et écris 4 phrases correspondant à ce que l'on doit ou ne doit pas faire.

1 

2 

3 

4 

1. ....
....

2. ....
....

3. ....
....

4. ....
....

Quick check

CD CLASSE

→ Manuel p. 57

1 **Écoute et trace l'itinéraire sur le plan ci-dessous.**

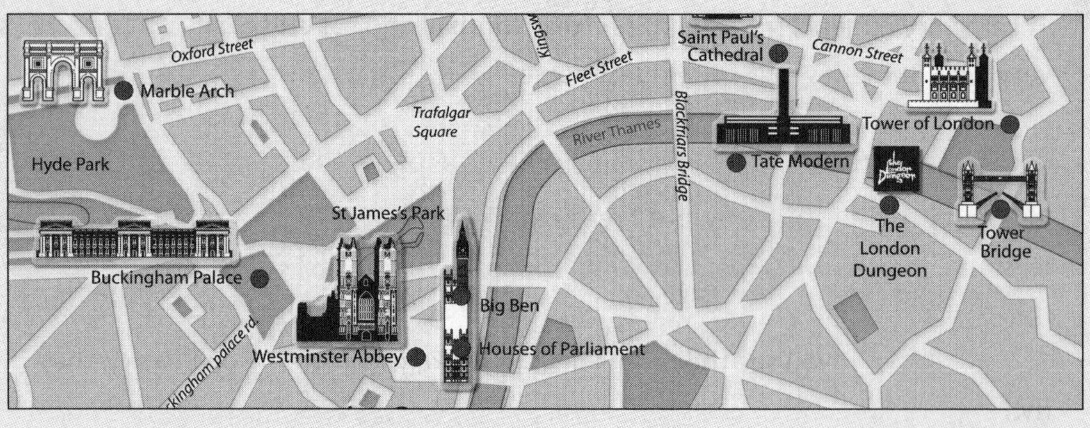

☐ **Je comprends un itinéraire et je sais l'expliquer.**

2 **Écoute et numérote les différentes parties du corps dans l'ordre où tu les entends.**

☐ **Je connais le vocabulaire des parties du corps.**

3 **Regarde les illustrations et dis ce que M. Smith est capable de faire ou pas.**

1 2 3

1. ....

2. ....

3. ....

☐ **Je sais dire ce que quelqu'un est capable de faire ou pas.**

My words

Les verbes

buy : acheter
decide : décider
go straight on : aller tout droit
I want / I don't want : je veux / je ne veux pas
turn left : tourner à gauche
turn right : tourner à droite
visit : visiter

Les adjectifs

beautiful : beau, belle
dangerous : dangereux(euse)
dark : sombre
famous : célèbre
scary : effrayant(e)

Les noms

a castle : un château
a crown : une couronne
ears : les oreilles
an eye : un œil
a finger : un doigt
a ghost : un fantôme
a head : la tête
a jewel : un bijou, un joyau
a king : un roi
a knee : un genou
a leg : une jambe
a mouth : la bouche
the night : la nuit
a nose : un nez
a painting : un tableau
the price : le prix
a queen : une reine
a raven : un corbeau
a shoulder : une épaule
a souvenir : un souvenir (*objet*)
a spider : une araignée
a toe : un orteil
a tooth (pluriel : teeth) **:** une dent
a tower : une tour
a visit : une visite

Les prépositions

behind : derrière
between : entre
in front of : devant

Les expressions

Have fun in London! : Profite bien de ton séjour à Londres !
how much? : combien ? (+ nom singulier)
how many? : combien ? (+ nom pluriel)
I don't care! : Je m'en moque !
there is : il y a (+ nom singulier)
there are : il y a (+ nom pluriel)

Maintenant je connais le lexique pour :

→ parler des parties du corps ☐ ☐ ☐
→ situer des objets ☐ ☐ ☐
→ donner des directions ☐ ☐ ☐
→ parler de monuments ☐ ☐ ☐

Check your progress

1 LISTEN

→ Manuel p. 61

An interesting visit

CD CLASSE

J'ai su :

A1

1. dire où se passe la visite, combien il y a de personnages et donner le prix de la visite. ....

2. expliquer ce qu'il faut ou ne faut pas faire pendant la visite.

A2

3. décrire la salle du château dont parle le guide. ....

2 READ

→ Manuel p. 61

A great monument

J'ai su :

A1

1. dire de quel monument il s'agit.

2. situer le monument (ville, quartier).

A1+

3. parler des informations pratiques (prix, horaires).

4. dire si le monument est célèbre.

3 SPEAK

→ Manuel p. 61

Meet the ghost!

J'ai su :

A1

- ☐ **1.** donner des informations sur son identité : nom et âge.

- ☐ **2.** décrire physiquement le fantôme.

A1+

- ☐ **3.** décrire ce qu'il est capable de faire ou pas.

- ☐ **4.** réagir et répondre aux questions de mes camarades.

4 WRITE

→ Manuel p. 61

A haunted castle

J'ai su :

A1

- ☐ **1.** donner des informations pratiques (prix, horaires).

A1+

- ☐ **2.** décrire ce qu'il y a à visiter dans le château.

- ☐ **3.** expliquer ce qu'il faut et ne faut pas faire pendant la visite.

Part 4 Family fun

Build up and organize your vocabulary

FAMILY MEMBERS

- a mother
- ……………………
- ……………………
- ……………………
- ……………………
- ……………………
- ……………………
- ……………………
- ……………………

FOOD AND DRINKS

- jelly
- ……………………
- ……………………
- ……………………
- ……………………
- ……………………
- ……………………
- ……………………
- ……………………

Family fun

PLACES IN A CITY

- a museum
- ……………………
- ……………………
- ……………………
- ……………………
- ……………………

HOBBIES

- play the guitar
- ……………………
- ……………………
- ……………………
- ……………………
- ……………………
- ……………………

MORE WORDS

- ……………………
- ……………………
- ……………………
- ……………………
- ……………………

Unit 7 What a family!

Discover

→ Manuel p. 66

Wordgym

CD CLASSE

b Listen for more information.
Complete the grid and speak about Andrew's family.

	Information
Andrew	
His sister	
His grandfather	
His grandmother	
His father	
His mother	
His uncle	
His aunt	

2

a Listen to the Sticklers' everyday life and number the pictures in chronological order.

CD CLASSE

b Say what time they do their different activities.

 ☐

 ☐

 ☐

 ☐

 ☐

 ☐

 ☐

Listen and speak

CD ÉLÈVE PISTE 10

→ Manuel p. 67

4 **a** **Look at the first picture in your book p. 67. Who can you see? Where are they? Are they happy?**

- Names: ....
- Place: ....
- Feelings: ....

....

....

b **Now listen and explain Chad's plans:** ....

....

....

....

My tactics

Écoute attentivement la première réplique de Chad. Découpe-la en groupes de mots. Quelles informations as-tu repérées ? ....

....

....

c **Now focus on Tom and Scarlett's reaction. Complete the grid below. Only write keywords.**

	Problems	Chad's suggestions
Scarlett	....	....
Tom	....	....

- **What is the children's final decision?**

....

....

....

d Listen to the second part of the conversation. Say who Chad speaks about and what the problem is.

....

....

e Listen carefully and find information about Chad's family.

Family members	Information
....	....
....	....
....	....

- **Comment on Scarlett and Tom's reaction.**

....

....

f Imagine a title for the story.

....

Store up your vocabulary

1. Note des actions que les personnages font toujours, parfois, souvent ou ne font jamais. ....

....

....

....

2. Note l'expression que Scarlett utilise pour parler de la famille de Chad.

....

3. Note le proverbe que la mère de Chad mentionne régulièrement :

"An apple ....

Grammar Memo

1. Pour parler de ce que quelqu'un fait **toujours**, j'emploie l'adverbe ....
2. Pour parler de ce qu'il fait **souvent**, j'emploie l'adverbe ....
3. Pour parler de ce qu'il fait **parfois**, j'emploie l'adverbe ....
4. Pour parler de ce qu'il ne fait **jamais**, j'emploie l'adverbe ....

⚠ Les adverbes de fréquence se placent .... le verbe.

Use what you know

→ Manuel p. 68

6 Speak for a minute

CD CLASSE

a Listen to Drake. Number the pictures in chronological order.

b Listen and complete the "Vampire Song".

He's .... up around midnight
He .... during the night
There he ...., there he ....
He's .... silent on tiptoe
He's .... silent on tiptoe
Tiptoe, tiptoe, tiptoe...

Watch out! The vampire ....!
.........................., you hear around midnight
Footsteps creaking in the night
Lock your door! There he ....!
There .... the vampire on tiptoe
There .... the vampire on tiptoe
Tiptoe, tiptoe, tiptoe...

Watch out! The vampire ....!
He .... makes a single noise
.... girls or boys
.... dreams of tender meat
Oh yes, he .... wants to eat
Oh yes he .... wants to eat
Sweet meat, sweet meat, sweet meat!
Watch out! The vampire ....!

Homework

Exercice 1

Fais six phrases pour dire si cela t'arrive souvent, parfois ou jamais de faire les choses suivantes pendant tes vacances.

1. get up late

....

2. play video games

....

3. play football

....

4. go to school

....

5. get up at 6 o'clock in the morning

....

6. watch TV

....

Exercice 2

Écris des phrases pour dire ce que Jake fait tous les jours à la même heure.

1 ◀ ....
....

.... ▶ 2
....

3 ◀ ....
....

.... ▶ 4
....

5 ◀ ....
....

.... ▶ 6
....

7 ◀ ....
....

.... ▶ 8
....

Quick check

→ Manuel p. 67

1 Écoute attentivement et écris à quelle heure Kevin fait les choses suivantes.

1. .... 2. .... 3. .... 4. .... 5. ....

☐ Je comprends l'heure en anglais.

2 Écoute et coche la case correspondant à ce que fait Kevin et à quelle fréquence.

	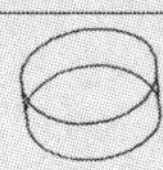	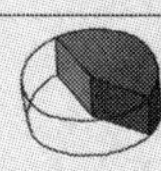	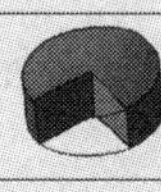	

☐ Je comprends des énoncés sur les habitudes de quelqu'un.

3 Utilise les informations que tu as repérées concernant Kevin et rédige en anglais quelques phrases sur ses habitudes.

....

....

....

....

....

☐ Je sais rédiger des énoncés sur le quotidien de quelqu'un.

Part 4

Unit 8 A picnic in Canterbury

Discover

Manuel p. 72

Wordgym

a **Write all the words you know about food.**

....

....

b **Then complete the grid below.**

Meat	Vegetables & fruit	Drinks	Sweets

2 **Match the things with the right people.** CD CLASSE

Listen and speak

CD ÉLÈVE PISTE 11 → Manuel p. 73

4 **a** **Look at the first picture in your book p. 73. Who can you see? Where are they? Are they happy? Angry? Embarrassed?**

- Names: ....
- Place: ....
- Feelings: ....

....

b **Listen to the beginning of the conversation and focus on Chad's mother. What is the conversation about?**

My tactics

- **Quels mots importants as-tu repérés dans les premières répliques ? Te permettent-ils de déduire de quoi il est question ?**

....

....

- **Repère deux questions que pose la mère de Chad. Entraîne-toi à repérer le pronom interrogatif. Peux-tu en déduire le sujet de la conversation ?**

....

....

....

c **Match the things with the correct people.**

• Mr O'Malley •
• Chad's brother •

d **Listen again and focus on Chad's brother. What is his problem?**

My tactics

Quel verbe le frère de Chad emploie t-il à plusieurs reprises ? Que peux-tu en déduire ?

....

....

Tick the food he mentions.

 ☐
 ☐

☐
 ☐

 ☐
 ☐
 ☐

e Listen to the rest of the conversation and look at pictures 3, 4 and 5 (book p. 73). Who can you see? Where are they? Are they happy? Angry? Impressed? Disappointed?

- Names: ....
- Place: ....
- Feelings: ....

....

f Listen and tick the things they see. Then speak about the children's reactions.

 ☐
 ☐
 ☐
 ☐

g Listen to the end. Do you think it is a funny ending? A sad ending?

....

h Imagine a title for the story.

....

Store up your vocabulary

- **Note deux phrases qui expriment ce que les personnages veulent faire.**

1. ....
2. ....

- **Note les deux questions que pose la mère de Chad au début de la conversation.**

3. ....
4. ....

Use what you know

→ Manuel p. 74

7 YOUR TASK

Write a short dialogue and act it out.

1. Make a list of the characters.

....

....

....

2. Make a list of Tom's mother's problems.

....

....

....

....

....

....

3. Write the dialogue:

....

....

....

....

....

....

Grammar Memo

- Pour demander à qui appartient un objet, j'utilise le pronom interrogatif : ....

Ex. : .... ?

- Pour parler de la possession en anglais, j'utilise le marqueur de génitif : ....

Ex. : .... ?

Homework

Exercice 1

Pose les questions correspondant aux réponses données.

1. ....? It's Peter's lunchbox.
2. ....? They are my father's keys.
3. ....? It is my mother's mobile phone.
4. ....? Paul and the children are in the cathedral.
5. ....? I think this boy is Kevin's friend.

Exercice 2

Traduis les phrases suivantes en anglais.

1. Mme O'Malley n'aime pas les chips de Scarlett.

....

2. Les clés du père de Tom sont dans la voiture.

....

3. Le téléphone portable de la mère de Tom est dans le sac de son frère.

....

4. L'ordinateur de Tom est dans la chambre de Zoe.

....

5. Chad aime bien les livres de Tom et de Zoe.

....

Exercice 3

Voici le début de l'histoire *A picnic in Canterbury*. Réécris-la en changeant le nom des aliments.

MRS O'MALLEY – Oh what a mess! Wait, whose carrot juice is this?
MR O'MALLEY – It's my carrot juice, darling.
CHAD'S BROTHER – Mum, I want my jelly…
MRS O'MALLEY– Wait a minute! You must eat your vegetables first… And whose… Oh, whose, whose crisps are these?
SCARLETT – They are mine Mrs O'Malley.
CHAD'S BROTHER – Mum, I want crisps too! I don't want vegetables! I want ham and I want sausages! I want chocolate cake!
MRS O'MALLEY – Oh, stop it! Eat your carrot and be quiet!

MRS O'MALLEY – ....
....
MR O'MALLEY – ....
....
CHAD'S BROTHER – ....
....
MRS O'MALLEY – ....
....
SCARLETT – ....
....
CHAD'S BROTHER – ....
....
....
MRS O'MALLEY – ....
....

Quick check

CD CLASSE → Manuel p. 73

1 **Écoute et dis s'il s'agit d'exclamations ou de questions.**

	Exclamation	Question
Phrase 1	☐	☐
Phrase 2	☐	☐
Phrase 3	☐	☐
Phrase 4	☐	☐
Phrase 5	☐	☐

☐ **Je sais différencier une question d'une exclamation.**

2 **Écoute et dis ce que veulent ou ne veulent pas faire les personnages suivants (prends des notes et rédige ensuite une phrase complète en anglais).**

1. Tom ....
2. Molly ....
3. Jake ....
4. Jack ....
5. Cathy ....

☐ **Je comprends ce que veulent des personnes.**

3 **Mr Lloyd n'est pas content car la salle de classe n'est pas rangée. Il ne sait pas à qui appartient les objets suivants : une trousse bleue, des chips, une bouteille d'eau, un ballon, des clés.**
John l'aide en lui donnant le nom des propriétaires. Rédige le dialogue.

Mr Lloyd: John, tell me… Whose ....?

John: I know… it's ....

....

....

....

....

....

....

☐ **Je sais demander et dire à qui appartient quelque chose.**

Part 4

Unit 9 We had a great time!

Discover

→ Manuel p. 78

Wordgym

a Read the definition.
A bookshop is a place where you can buy books.

b Now complete the definition using the following words.

Use: buy eat watch swim drink sleep

1. A restaurant is a place where ……………………………
2. A hotel ……………………………
3. A supermarket ……………………………
4. A cinema ……………………………
5. A swimming-pool ……………………………

2 Listen and speak about Matt and Jodie's great visit. CD CLASSE

a Say where Matt and Jodie are...

... today: ……………………………

• **Say where Matt and Jodie were...**

... yesterday: ……………………………

b What did they do yesterday? Did they like their visit? Complete the grid below.

Activities	Impressions, reactions, feelings
……………………	……………………
……………………	……………………
……………………	……………………
……………………	……………………
……………………	……………………

Read and speak

→ Manuel p. 79

4 **a** **Complete the different parts of the document in French.**

....

From: scarlettwilliams@myworld.com

to: kevinwilliams@yahoo.com ....

Object: A crazy weekend ....

Dear Dad, ...

....

I had a very strange weekend. On Saturday, Chad invited me to a picnic party with his family. We went to Canterbury. His family is a bit strange! His mother ate carrots and drank tomato juice! I didn't eat carrots! I had crisps! Chad's uncle, Paul, said there was a treasure in the cathedral. The treasure of the Black Prince. He wanted to find it. So Paul, Chad and Tom went to explore the cathedral. They didn't find any treasure, but they saw the Black Prince's tomb and the place where Thomas Becket was executed. They decided to go down into the crypt, but Paul fell down the stairs and he broke his leg! We called an ambulance. The ambulance took Paul to hospital. It was a crazy day with a crazy family but we had fun! It was a great day!

And how are you? How is everything in New York? Did you have a nice weekend? Did you go to Central Park? Please write soon. I miss you.

Love,

Scarlett. ....

....

My tactics

Tu as repéré à quoi correspondent les différentes zones du texte.
Déduis-en :

- la nature du document : ....
- le nom de l'auteur : ....
- à qui il est adressé ....

b **Read the document. Circle the verbs. Underline the key sentences.**

My tactics

Repère bien les verbes dans le texte. À quel temps sont-ils ? Que peux-tu en déduire ?

....

Then say what the e-mail is about. ....

c Make a list of the characters mentioned in the text. Write down information about them.

My tactics

Certains mots ressemblent au français et t'aident à mieux comprendre les informations d'un document. Relis le texte et recopie les mots transparents.

....

....

....

Characters' names	Who are they?	Information
Scarlett	Chad's friend	....
....	....	....
....	....	....
....	....	....
....	....	....

Historical characters	Names and information
....	....
....	....

d Now say if these sentences are right or wrong. Justify your answers.

	right	wrong
1. Scarlett wrote a nice letter to her father.	☐	☐
2. Scarlett's weekend was not interesting.	☐	☐
3. Chad's mother ate a delicious ham sandwich at the picnic.	☐	☐
4. Tom, Chad and Paul visited the Tower of London.	☐	☐
5. At the end of the visit, Paul had an accident.	☐	☐

Grammar Memo

- Pour parler du passé en anglais, j'utilise le ....
- Pour conjuguer un verbe régulier au passé, j'ajoute .... au verbe.
- À la forme négative, j'utilise l'auxiliaire .... suivi du verbe à ....
- Pour poser une question au passé, j'utilise l'auxiliaire ....

Use what you know

→ Manuel p. 80

6 Speak in pairs

The class interviews a pupil about his weekend.

a Make a list of the verbs you can use to ask questions.

....

....

....

b Now ask your questions and complete the following grid.

***You*: Did you....** ***Pupil*: Yes, I did – No, I didn't**

YES	NO
....	....
....	....
....	....
....	....

c Now recap and write a paragraph about your friend's weekend.

....

....

....

....

Homework

Exercice 1 **Utilise les illustrations pour dire où ces personnes étaient hier.**

1. ....

2. ....

3. ....

4. ....

5. ....

Exercice 2 **Dis ce que Mr Davis a fait et n'a pas fait pendant son week-end. Utilise les informations du tableau pour rédiger un paragraphe.**

Yes	No
London	swimming-pool
Westminster Abbey	video games
restaurant	tennis
cinema	Saint Paul's Cathedral
Tower of London	Hyde Park

....
....
....
....
....
....
....
....
....

Quick check

→ Manuel p. 79

1 Écoute les cinq définitions suivantes et dis de quoi il s'agit.

a. ....

b. ....

c. ....

d. ....

e. ....

☐ **Je suis capable de comprendre des définitions.**

2 Lis l'e-mail ci-dessous et fais-en un résumé.

From: sam.kerry@yahoo.com
to: george-kerry@hotmail.com
Object: Great weekend

Dear Dad,
I had a really good weekend! I went to New York with Aunt Anna and Uncle Harry. We had a great time. We visited the statue of Liberty. We went up the Empire State Building. We had a picnic in Central Park. I ate chips and a hotdog. I played football with Uncle Harry. We had lots of fun! We didn't have time to visit the Metropolitan Museum of Art, but on Saturday night, we went to the theater on Broadway. We stayed in a really nice hotel. My room was wonderful! What about you Dad? Did you have a nice weekend in London? When are you coming back to Washington?
Love, Sam.

....

....

....

....

....

☐ **Je comprends un e-mail racontant les activités d'un week-end.**

3 Écris 3 phrases pour dire ce que tu as fait le week-end dernier.

a. ....

b. ....

c. ....

☐ **Je sais raconter ce que j'ai fait à un moment du passé.**

My words

Les verbes

drink (drank) : boire
eat (ate) : manger
get up (got up) : se lever
go (went) : aller
have fun (had fun) : bien s'amuser
play : jouer
see (saw) : voir
sleep (slept) : dormir
wash : laver
watch : regarder

Les adjectifs

fantastic : fantastique
great : super
healthy : bon pour la santé
impressive : impressionnant(e)
wonderful : merveilleux(euse)

Les noms

an apple : une pomme
an aunt : une tante
a brother : un frère
a carrot : une carotte
cheese : le fromage
chocolate cake : du gâteau au chocolat
a cousin : un cousin, une cousine
crisps : des chips
a father : un père
a grandfather : un grand-père
a grandmother : une grand-mère
ham : du jambon
jelly : gelée (dessert anglais)
juice : du jus
meat : la viande
a mother : une mère
sausages : des saucisses
a sister : une sœur
a tomato : une tomate
an uncle : un oncle
vegetables : les légumes

Les adverbes

always : toujours
never : jamais
often : souvent
sometimes : parfois

Maintenant je connais :

→ quelques verbes au présent et au prétérit ☐ ☐ ☐
→ les adverbes de fréquence ☐ ☐ ☐
→ le lexique de la famille et de la nourriture ☐ ☐ ☐

Part 4

Check your progress

1 LISTEN

→ Manuel p. 83

Lost and found

J'ai su :

A1 ☐ **1.** dire où se passe la scène, combien il y a de personnages.

....

....

....

A1+ ☐ **2.** dire de quels objets l'on parle.

....

....

....

☐ **3.** repérer à qui appartient chaque objet mentionné.

....

....

....

2 READ

→ Manuel p. 83

Dover Castle

J'ai su :

A1 ☐ **1.** dire qui a écrit la carte et à qui elle est adressée.

....

A1+ ☐ **2.** dire brièvement ce dont on parle dans la carte postale.

....

....

A2 ☐ **3.** décrire en détail les événements racontés dans la carte postale.

....

....

3 SPEAK

→ Manuel p. 83

A businessman's life

J'ai su :

A1 ☐ **1.** donner des informations sur l'identité de M. Duncan : nom, métier.

....

....

A1+ ☐ **2.** décrire avec des phrases simples quelques activités de M. Duncan.

....

....

A2 ☐ **3.** décrire en détail les activités de M. Duncan, en en précisant les heures, et en reliant les phrases avec *and* ou *but.*

....

....

4 WRITE

→ Manuel p. 83

A day in Canterbury

J'ai su :

A1 ☐ **1.** présenter correctement la carte postale.

....

....

....

....

A1+ ☐ **2.** écrire quelques phrases sur Canterbury.

....

A2 ☐ **3.** décrire en détail ce que j'ai fait, les monuments que j'ai visités, ce que j'ai mangé et où. Dire si j'ai aimé ou pas.

....

....

....

Part 5 Show time

Build up and organize your vocabulary

Show time

PERSONALITY
- funny
- ....
- ....
- ....
- ....
- ....

PHYSICAL APPEARANCE
- tall
- ....
- ....
- ....
- ....
- ....

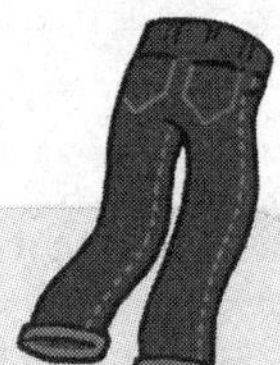

CLOTHES
- trousers
- ....
- ....
- ....
- ....
- ....
- ....

AT THE THEATRE
- an actor
- ....
- ....
- ....
- ....
- ....

ACCESSORIES
- a belt
- ....
- ....
- ....
- ....
- ....

MORE WORDS
- ....
- ....
- ....
- ....
- ....

Part 5

Unit 10 Time to act

Discover

→ Manuel p. 88

Wordgym

Look at the picture and write a sentence to describe each character.

small fat slim naughty nice intelligent stupid

1. ....
2. ....
3. ....
4. ....
5. ....
6. ....
7. ....

2 Listen to Jackson Jones and tick the qualities of each actor. CD CLASSE

	Brad	Tom	Jack
more elegant			
taller			
shorter			
more athletic			
stronger			
more intelligent			

Now write the name of each actor under his picture.

....

Listen and speak

CD ÉLÈVE PISTE 13

→ Manuel p. 89

4 **a Listen to the beginning of the conversation and find information about Mrs Monroe's show.**

- **Name of the show:** ....
- **Name of the characters:** ....

b Listen to the rest of the conversation. Find information about:

- Mrs Monroe's plans: ....
- Scarlett wants to be: ....
- Tom wants to be: ....
- Chad wants to be: ....
- Mrs Monroe must choose between .... and ....

c Read the list of adjectives below. Then listen again and tick.

My tactics

Note les mots accentués et le ton des personnages, ils t'aideront à trouver la bonne réponse.

....

....

....

Qualities for the role	Tom	Chad
tall	☐	☐
funny	☐	☐
good-looking	☐	☐
athletic	☐	☐
hard-working	☐	☐
good memory	☐	☐
romantic	☐	☐
good at dancing	☐	☐
good at acting	☐	☐

Now recap:

- What are Chad's qualities for the role?

....

....

- What are Tom's qualities for the role?

....

....

Scarlett prefers .... because she thinks he is ....

Imagine a title: ....

Store up your vocabulary

Note 3 adjectifs qualificatifs pour chaque catégorie.

1. Description physique : ....

....

2. Description psychologique : ....

....

Grammar Memo

Observe les comparaisons suivantes:

1. *I'm more intelligent than Jake and I'm more athletic.*
2. *I'm taller and I'm stronger.*
3. *Chad is funnier than Tom.*

Souligne les adjectifs dans ces phrases puis complète le tableau.

Comparatif	Adjectif de base	Nombre de syllabes de l'adjectif	Formation du comparatif
more intelligent	intelligent	4	more + intelligent
more athletic	....	....	....
taller	....	....	....
stronger	....	....	....
funnier	....	....	....

Use what you know

→ Manuel p. 90

6 Speak for a minute

Character's name	Appearance and personality
....	....
....	....

- **Matt's favourite character:** ....
- **Film title:** ....

7 YOUR TASK

Before your audition, prepare your arguments:

My qualities for the role	Why I am better
Ex.: good memory	I have a better memory than the others: I can remember ....
....	....
....	....
....	....
....	....

Homework

Exercice 1

Tu es au cirque. Écris quatre phrases pour comparer le clown Marcus avec les autres clowns. ***Ex.:*** Marcus is taller than Ziggy.

1. ....

2. ....

3. ....

4. ....

Exercice 2

Remplis cette grille de mots croisés avec le contraire de chaque mot donné.

1. ugly
2. thin
3. small
4. serious
5. weak
6. stupid

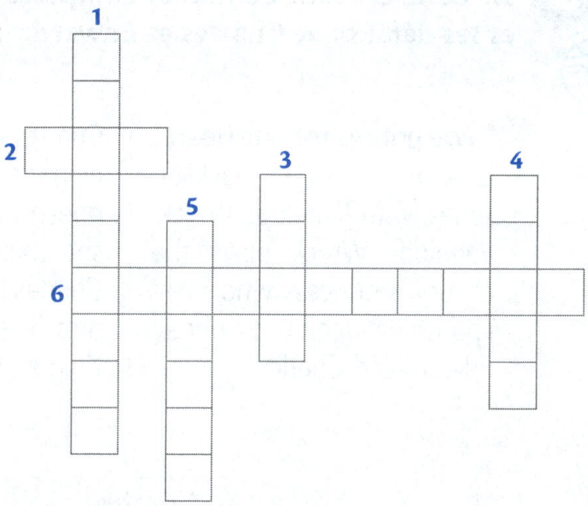

Exercice 3

Dessine Jack et Jones à partir des informations ci-dessous :

1. Jack is taller than Jones but Jones is stronger than Jack.
2. Jack's hat is bigger than Jones's hat.
3. Jones is funnier: he always smiles.

Jack	Jones

Quick check

→ Manuel p. 89

2 **Après une audition, le metteur en scène et le producteur discutent de leur acteur préféré. Écoute et trouve les qualités des candidats.**

Lucy	Shirley
....	....
....	....
....	....

Jack prefers: ....

Caroline prefers: ....

☐ **Dans une conversation, je peux comprendre la décision d'une personne et ses arguments.**

3 **Lis cette critique de film et complète le tableau pour repérer les qualités et les défauts de Charles et Edward.**

"**Two princes for One Heart**" is a new film by Jackson Jones, with Penelope Wreck. Penelope Wreck plays the role of a princess who must choose between two princes: Edward and Charles. Charles is stronger and more elegant, but the princess doesn't like him because she thinks he's pretentious. Charles is richer than Edward, and he's better looking. The King and the Queen want the princess to marry Charles but the princess thinks Edward is funnier and more sensitive. Who will the princess marry in the end? Will she be happy? Don't miss "Two Princes for One Heart".

Charles	Edward
rich	....
....	....
....	....
....	....
....	....
....	....

Que peux-tu en conclure ?

The princess's choice is ....

☐ **Je peux repérer les qualités des personnages dans un texte.**
Je peux comprendre le choix d'une personne ainsi que ses arguments.

Part 5

Unit 11 Get ready for the show

Discover

→ Manuel p. 94

Wordgym

Who is who? Write the name under each person.

1. Lucy is wearing a skirt and a cap.
2. John is wearing a sweater and a white pair of shoes.
3. Mark is wearing a black T-shirt and a jacket.
4. Mary is wearing a tracksuit.

....

3 **Listen and number the pictures in the right order. Then complete the sentences.**

"I'm .... " "I'm .... " "I'm .... "

Listen and speak

CD ÉLÈVE PISTE 14 → Manuel p. 95

4 **a** **What are the boys doing? What are their problems?**

How does Mrs Monroe react?

My tactics

Quelles formes verbales en *-ing* entends-tu ? À quelle action et à quel sentiment sont-elles associées ?

....

....

actions	sentiments
....	....
....	....

Now fill in the grid.

	Tom	Chad
his action	....	....
his problem	....	....
Mrs Monroe's reaction	....	....

b **What is Mrs Monroe's problem?**

Write down the keywords:

....

Discuss with the class and write a sentence:

....

....

c **Listen to the end of the conversation.**

What is Scarlett doing? ....

Who is calling her? Fill in the grid.

Name: ....

Place: ....

Why he is calling: ....

....

Store up your vocabulary

Écoute à nouveau le dialogue et repère les expressions utiles dans un magasin de vêtements :

1. ....
2. ....
3. ....
4. ....
5. ....

Grammar Memo

a Observe les phrases suivantes :

1. *What are you doing?*
2. *I'm putting on my trousers.*
3. *She isn't speaking on the phone.*

Ces phrases décrivent :

☐ des habitudes ☐ des événements passés ☐ des actions en cours au moment où l'on parle

b Complète le tableau.

Forme affirmative	Forme interrogative	Forme négative
Sujet + *be* + base verbale + *-ing*	.... + sujet + ... + *-ing* ?	Sujet + ... + *not* + ... + ...

Use what you know

Manuel p. 96

6 Speak for a minute

Prepare your excuses!
Look at your book (p. 96) and prepare a list of verbs for each situation.

A ....

B ....

C ....

D ....

7 YOUR TASK

Do a live report.
Look at your book (p. 96) and make notes on the people's actions to prepare your report.

People	Actions
The actress (the girl with the yellow dress)	
The dancers (the man with the green trousers and the man with the blue shirt)	
The decorator (the man with the green cap)	
The main actor (the boy with the orange T-shirt)	
The choreographer (the woman in pink)	

Homework

Exercice 1 **Décris ce que ces personnes sont en train de faire.**

1

2

3

4

5

6

7

1. ....
2. ....
3. ....
4. ....
5. ....
6. ....
7. ....

Exercice 2 **Relis le script de la conversation (manuel p. 152) et complète la conversation téléphonique de Mrs Monroe avec Kevin, le père de Scarlett.**

MRS MONROE: Hello?

KEVIN: ....?

MRS MONROE: No, I'm not Scarlett's friend! I'm Scarlett's teacher!

KEVIN: ....?

MRS MONROE: No, we are not at school, we're in a shop!

KEVIN: ....?

MRS MONROE: We're buying the costumes for the show!

KEVIN: ....?

MRS MONROE: What? No, we're not having fun!

Quick check

→ Manuel p. 95

1 Écoute ces descriptions et dis de quelle personne il s'agit.

....

☐ Je sais identifier quelqu'un à partir de la description de ses vêtements.

2 Décris chacun de ces personnages en deux phrases : une phrase décrivant ce qu'il porte et une autre décrivant ce qu'il est en train de faire.

1. ....

....

2. ....

....

☐ Je sais décrire les vêtements de quelqu'un.
Je peux dire ce que quelqu'un est en train de faire.

3 Lis cette description des parents de ton correspondant et classe les habitudes et les actions en cours.

My dad works in a bank but he is not working at the moment, he's on holidays and he's renovating the house. He loves DIY, he often repairs objects and renovate things. My mum's a French teacher. She teaches French and she's learning Spanish at the moment. My sister's a star! She goes to dance school everyday and today they are going to Leeds to perform their new musical.

	Habitudes	Actions en cours
father	....	....
mother	....	....
sister	....	....

☐ Je sais distinguer une habitude d'une action en cours.

Part 5

Unit 12 A great musical

Discover

→ Manuel p. 100

Wordgym

Classify these words about show business: actions, people or places?

actor act dancer
sing singer director
theatre cinema superstar
dance audience

Actions	People	Places
....	....	....
....	....	....
....	....	....
....	....	....
....	....	....

2 **a Listen to the interview and say who Julia is speaking about:** CD CLASSE

....

....

b What was the most horrible thing Julia had to do?

....

....

Read and speak

→ Manuel p. 101

4 **a** **Give information about the document.**

My tactics

Note des éléments de la mise en page (le titre et l'illustration du document) qui te permettent d'anticiper son contenu.

....

....

De quoi ce texte va-t-il parler ?

....

- What type of document is it?

  ☐ a passage from a novel ☐ a comic strip ☐ an article

- Who is the writer? ....
- What is the topic? ....

b **Read and find information about the show.**

- Name of the actors: ....
- Name of the director: ....
- Place of the show: ....
- Waiting time to buy the tickets: ....
- The audience's impression after the show: ....

c **Say if the sentences on p. 95 are right or wrong.**

My tactics

Repère bien à qui se réfèrent les pronoms personnels pour éviter les confusions.

1. **She** told **us**. → **she** = ... **us** = ...
2. A lot of people already admire **her**. → **her** = ...
3. **She** had to sing with **him**. → **she** = ... **him** = ...
4. **She** told **them**. → **she** = ... **them** = ...

	right	wrong
1. There were a lot of spectators.	☐	☐
2. Chad knew his text very well.	☐	☐
3. Now Scarlett has got a lot of fans.	☐	☐
4. Scarlett did not really prepare for the show.	☐	☐
5. Scarlett enjoyed the experience: it was fun and easy.	☐	☐
6. Mrs Monroe was a bit disappointed.	☐	☐

• **Now write a sentence from the article to justify.**

....

• **Imagine a title for this document:**

....

Grammar Memo

a Observe les phrases suivantes et souligne le verbe de chacune d'elles.

1. *I had to learn a lot of pages.*
2. *We had to exercise a lot.*
3. *His teacher had to come on stage to help him.*

Quelle expression précède le verbe ? ....

Qu'exprime cette expression ?

☐ une obligation passée
☐ une interdiction passée
☐ une permission passée

b Complète :

.... + base verbale, permet d'exprimer une ....
Au passé, elle remplace l'auxiliaire modal ....

Use what you know

→ Manuel p. 102

5 Write a few lines

You're a journalist. There are too many repetitions in this article! Replace the nouns with pronouns.

High School musical is a love story between Troy and Gabriella. .... meet during a holiday. Troy sings a karaoke with Gabriella and .... thinks .... is fantastic. When Troy goes back to school .... sees Gabriella again, ... is a new pupil. .... meets Troy's friends, Sharpay and Ryan. Sharpay asks Troy "Do you want to be in the show with ...."? When Sharpay discovers that Gabriella can sing better than ...., ... becomes furious…

6 Speak for a minute

Mrs Monroe had a very busy day. She had to prepare the show.

a Look at the drawing and make a list of the clothes and accessories.

1. ....
2. ....
3. ....
4. ....
5. ....
6. ....

b Read her diary and say what she had to do:

- In the morning: ....
....
- In the afternoon: ....
....

Homework

Exercice 1

Relis l'article (livre page 101) et dis à qui se réfèrent les pronoms soulignés.

1. A lot of people in Kingston already admire her.

Her = ...

2. She had to sing with him.

She = ... him = ...

3. His teacher had to come and help him.

him = ...

4. She said to them: "This was a great evening for me".

She .... them = ... me = ...

Exercice 2

Retrouve huit mots liés au monde du spectacle.

T	V	A	L	Q	G	Q	M	G	O	S	U	M	K	A
A	U	D	I	E	N	C	E	U	T	C	K	C	N	C
E	A	Y	B	H	S	C	C	A	S	D	A	G	P	T
K	W	S	O	U	F	L	G	F	Q	I	Q	I	G	O
V	K	D	O	T	G	E	J	E	O	R	C	H	A	R
D	Y	K	Z	G	U	V	K	K	G	E	Q	A	J	S
H	B	V	L	Z	O	X	P	T	M	C	L	I	L	K
S	D	O	A	H	S	J	F	H	Z	T	A	F	M	Z
U	H	U	J	B	S	W	Y	E	G	O	S	K	V	Z
P	X	O	K	L	V	P	G	A	G	R	O	V	G	O
O	M	V	W	L	G	P	E	T	W	X	A	X	Y	A
V	B	R	J	J	P	E	P	R	F	F	Q	N	Z	V
J	P	V	F	V	L	U	U	E	U	X	J	A	S	N
P	H	G	E	B	A	S	M	W	W	X	J	F	F	B
T	W	F	P	Z	Y	C	Z	V	N	V	C	D	Z	N

- ACTOR
- DIRECTOR
- STAGE
- SHOW
- PLAY
- AUDIENCE
- THEATER
- MUSICAL

Exercice 3

Mr Jackson a passé une journée bien remplie. Décris tout ce qu'il a dû faire.

1

2

3

4

5

1. ....

2. ....

3. ....

4. ....

5. ....

Quick check

CD CLASSE → Manuel p. 101

1 **Lis les renseignements qui te sont donnés.**
Dis qui tu préfères et pourquoi. Puis explique les problèmes que chaque acteur a rencontrés et ce qu'il a dû faire.

Orlando Bloom
(UK)

Born in: 1974
Problems in life:
- dyslexia (solution: special lessons)
- 1988: bulimia (solution: diet for 7 years)
- 1995: paralysis after an accident (solution: do reeducation and sport)

Style: casual and simple

Johnny Depp
(USA)

Born in: 1963
Problems in life:
- he started very poor (solution: sell pens)
- he was the hero of a TV series and film directors did not take him seriously (solution: be original)
- 2006: his daughter was very ill (solution: stay a long time in hospital. Stop working)

Style: casual but sophisticated

....

....

....

....

....

☐ **Je sais exprimer une préférence à la lecture d'un texte et la justifier.**

2 **Écoute la conversation et complète la grille.**

Steve's favourite film	Lisa's favourite film
Arguments:	Arguments:
•	• ....
•	• ....
•	• ....

☐ **Dans une conversation, je peux comprendre ce que quelqu'un préfère et les arguments qu'il utilise.**

My words

Les adjectifs

athletic : athlétique
beautiful : beau, belle
big : gros (grosse), grand(e)
cheap : bon marché
expensive : cher, chère
fat : gros (grosse)
good-looking : beau, belle
hard-working : travailleur(euse)
intelligent : intelligent(e)
naughty : méchant(e)
pretty : beau, belle
short : court(e)
slim : mince
small : petit(e)
stupid : stupide, bête
tall : grand(e)
ugly : laid(e), vilain(e)

Les noms

• Show business

an actor : un acteur
an actress : une actrice
the audience : le public
a dancer : un danseur
a director : un metteur en scène
a film / a movie : un film
a play : une pièce
a rehearsal : une répétition
a show : un spectacle
a singer : un chanteur(euse)
a theatre : un théâtre

• Clothes

a cap : une casquette
a coat : un manteau
a dress : une robe
a hat : un chapeau
a jacket : une veste
(a pair of) trousers : un pantalon
a shirt : une chemise
a skirt : une jupe

Les verbes

act : jouer
dance : dancer
learn : apprendre
perform : interpréter
put on : mettre, enfiler (un vêtement)
sing : chanter
try on : essayer (un vêtement)

Les pronoms personnels compléments

her : elle
him : lui
me : moi
them : eux, elles, les
us : nous
you : toi, vous

Maintenant je connais :

→ les mots du monde du spectacle ☐ ☐ ☐
→ le lexique des vêtements ☐ ☐ ☐
→ les pronoms personnels compléments ☐ ☐ ☐

Part 5 Check your progress

1 LISTEN

→ Manuel p. 105

Which film is better?

CD CLASSE

J'ai su :

A1 ☐ **1.** comprendre le sujet général de l'interview.

....

A1+ ☐ **2.** dire lequel des deux films est une comédie.

....

....

A2 ☐ **3.** dire lequel des deux films John Cannon a préféré tourner et pourquoi.

....

....

2 READ

→ Manuel p. 105

A message from Mark

J'ai su :

A1 ☐ **1.** comprendre dans quel but Mark écrit cet e-mail.

....

A1+ ☐ **2.** comprendre pourquoi il n'a pas pu faire ce qu'il voulait.

....

....

A2 ☐ **3.** comprendre ce qu'il a dû faire à la place.

....

....

3 SPEAK

→ Manuel p. 105

What are they doing?

J'ai su :

A1 ☐ **1.** expliquer ce qui est en train de se passer.

A1+ ☐ **2.** donner des explications supplémentaires.

A2 ☐ **3.** réagir en faisant des commentaires sur ce qui se passe.

4 WRITE

→ Manuel p. 105

Toni, Sheila and the criminals

J'ai su :

A1 ☐ **1.** recopier le texte sans fautes.

A1+ ☐ **2.** raccourcir le texte et le clarifier en évitant les répétitions.

Part 6 Across the sea

Build up and organize your vocabulary

Across the sea

MEANS OF TRANSPORT

- ferry
- ....
- ....
- ....

LANDSCAPES

- sea
- ....
- ....
- ....
- ....
- ....

ACCOMMODATION

- hotel
- ....
- ....
- ....
- ....

VERBS OF MOVEMENT

- travel
- ....
- ....
- ....
- ....

MORE WORDS

- ....
- ....
- ....
- ....
- ....

Unit 13 Off to Ireland

Discover

→ Manuel p. 110

Wordgym

a **Find the missing letters.**

b **Match the means of transport with the places.**

Plane •	• Ha… bou…
Ca… •	• T… ain station
T… ain •	• Ca… pa… k
Fe… …y •	• C… ach st… ti… n
Co… ch •	• Ai… po… t

2 **Listen to the conversation and say what options Mr and Mrs Clarke have chosen.**

Transport	……………………………………
Accommodation	……………………………………
Package: **Tick the name of the package and say what it includes.**	☐ "Magic Ireland" ☐ "Romantic Ireland" ☐ "Incredible Ireland"
Price	……………………………………

3 **Listen and fill in the grid.**

	Past	Future	Keywords
1	……………	……………	……………
2	……………	……………	……………
3	……………	……………	……………
4	……………	……………	……………
5	……………	……………	……………

Listen and speak

CD ÉLÈVE PISTE 16

→ Manuel p. 111

4 **a** **Listen to the beginning of the conversation. Say where the characters are and where they are going.**

My tactics

Repère les indications de lieu qui peuvent t'aider et note-les ici.

....

....

Destination: ....

Means of transport: ....

b **Reasons for the trip: choose two answers and justify by writing one sentence from the script.**

☐ tourism ☐ family visit ☐ school trip ☐ rugby match

....

....

c **Choose two titles for the first part.**

☐ A kind invitation. ☐ A dangerous trip.

☐ Chad's grandmother. ☐ Off to Ireland.

d **Listen again to the conversation and find information about the old lady.**

My tactics

Repère les indications de temps et note-les ici.

....

Font-elles référence au passé ou à l'avenir ? ....

- First name ....
- Age ....
- Country of origin ....
- Favourite means of transport ....

- Favourite kind of snack ....
- Name of her first love ....
- Place of her first love ....

e **Listen to the end of the conversation and tick the right picture.**

 ☐

 ☐

Store up your vocabulary

Note ici tout ce que Chad, Tom et Scarlett veulent visiter en Irlande :

....

....

....

Grammar Memo

a **Observe les phrases suivantes.**

1. *You should listen to my story.*

2. *I'd like some tea.*

Quelle phrase exprime un souhait ? ....

Quelle phrase exprime une recommandation ? ....

b **Complète.**

Pour parler de ce que j'aimerais faire, j'utilise l'expression « .... like » suivie d'un **groupe nominal** ou de ***to* + base verbale.**

Pour parler de ce que je devrais faire, j'utilise « .... » suivi de la **base verbale.**

Use what you know

→ Manuel p. 112

5 Speak in pairs

Prepare the dialogue. Fill in the grid.

You	Your friend
What you would like to see: **1.** .... because .... **2.** .... because .... **3.** .... because	**What he/she would like to see:** **1.** .... because .... **2.** .... because .... **3.** .... because ....
Where you would like to stay: **1.** .... because .... **2.** .... because	**Where he/she would like to stay:** **1.** .... because .... **2.** .... because ....

6 YOUR TASK

Write an e-mail to the Tourism Board of Ireland to ask for some information.

From: ....

to: information@discoverireland.com

Object: ....

Dear Sir or Madam,

I'd like to ....

....

Can you ....

Thank you for your kind attention.

Yours faithfully, ...

Homework

Exercice 1

Reformule ces cinq exclamations en utilisant « what ».

1. This lake is so beautiful!

....

2. That castle is so big!

....

3. This lady is so nice!

....

4. Your story is so romantic.

....

5. This man is so gallant!

....

Exercice 2

Comment dirais-tu en anglais :

1. Vous devriez visiter le stade de Dublin.

....

2. Vous devriez aller à un concert.

....

3. J'aimerais aller voir la mer.

....

4. Scarlett aimerait visiter un château.

....

5. Rose voudrait du thé.

....

Exercice 3

Retrouve dans la grille sept moyens de transport.

BICYCLE
CAR
TRAIN
BOAT
FERRY
BUS
PLANE

B	P	X	Q	R	D	E	Z	M	G
M	I	L	Q	A	G	C	Q	J	T
T	L	C	A	C	O	K	E	H	Z
S	Q	L	Y	N	N	I	A	R	T
X	U	E	F	C	E	N	M	J	A
B	A	B	L	Z	L	R	V	G	G
G	K	Z	R	L	Q	E	B	M	X
F	E	R	R	Y	T	A	O	B	V
E	I	B	O	M	I	V	J	B	Q
Y	Y	U	F	C	I	K	N	Z	M

Quick check

→ Manuel p. 111

1 Écoute la conversation et complète la grille.

What Mr Simpson wants to see	What Mrs Simpson wants to see
....	....
....	....

What do they finally decide?

....

☐ Dans une conversation, je sais reconnaître les souhaits et les choix des personnes qui parlent.

2 Tom et Scarlett ont noté ce qu'ils aimeraient faire lors de leur voyage. Écris six phrases exprimant leurs souhaits.

Scarlett: go shopping / visit Bunratty castle / go horse-riding
Tom: see a rugby match / go to a concert / visit Bunratty castle

1. ....
2. ....
3. ....
4. ....
5. ....
6. ....

☐ Je sais formuler par écrit ce que quelqu'un aimerait faire.

3 Lis cette brochure de Bunratty Castle et associe les recommandations aux panneaux.

Welcome to Bunratty Castle and historical village!

Here are a few tips for you to enjoy your visit

1. You should visit our information centre: our hostesses will help you to organize your visit.

2. When you visit the farm, you should not give food to the animals.

3. Be careful in the castle: children and elderly visitors should not go up the tower, as it can be difficult.

4. Before leaving, you should visit our traditional shop and its unique collection of Irish jerseys.

 ☐

 ☐

 ☐

 ☐

☐ Je sais comprendre des recommandations écrites.

Unit 14 The magic island

Discover

→ Manuel p. 116

Wordgym

Look at your book p.116 for one minute and remember the words. Then close your book and complete this map.

1. ....
2. ....
3. ....
4. ....
5. ....
6. ....
7. ....
8. ....
9. ....
10. ....
11. ....

2 **Read the text and put the pictures in the right order. Then write a caption under each picture.**

☐ 
....
....

☐ 
....
....

☐ 
....
....

☐ 
....
....

☐ 
....
....

3 **Listen and match the years with the drawings.** CD CLASSE

1. around 1915 **2.** around 1935 **3.** around 1940 **4.** the day before yesterday

 ☐

☐

 ☐

 ☐

Listen and speak

CD ÉLÈVE PISTE 17

→ Manuel p. 117

4 **a** **Listen to the beginning of the conversation and find information about the place 1 and the characters 2 3.**

My tactics

Repère et note les dates et les indications de durée et « *ago* ».
Puis associe-les aux événements auxquels ils se rapportent.

....

....

....

1 

....

....

....

....

2 

....

....

....

....

3 

....

....

....

....

b **Listen to the rest of the conversation. Focus on Rose's questions.**

My tactics

Écoute bien le premier mot de chaque question (le mot en WH-).
Note ici tous les mots interrogatifs en WH- que tu connais :

....

....

....

Write down three of Rose's questions.

.... ?

.... ?

.... ?

c Listen again and focus on Danny's answers. Find three justifications.

1. ....
2. ....
3. ....

d Choose the best title for the dialogue.

☐ Lady and the tramp ☐ What a lovely house! ☐ Eternal Love

Store up your vocabulary

Complète toutes les unités de temps, de la plus petite à la plus grande :

1. a second
2. a m..........................
3. an h..........................
4. a d..........................
5. a w..........................
6. a m..........................
7. a y..........................
8. a c..........................

Grammar Memo

1 Observe les phrases suivantes et souligne les indications de durée.

a. *I was born 83 years ago.*

b. *My family bought the house a century ago.*

c. *We arrived two days ago.*

2 Complète:

.................., placé en fin de phrase, sert à exprimer la .... qui s'est écoulée entre un événement passé et le moment où je parle. Il est toujours précédé d'un ....

Use what you know

→ Manuel p. 118

5 Speak in pairs

Prepare questions to your friend.
Then write the answers and find which famous Irishman it is.

Date of birth	**Q.** When ....? **A.** ....
Place of birth	**Q.** Where..? **A.** ....
Place where he started his career	**Q.** ....? **A.** ....
Year when he started his career	**Q.** ....? **A.** ....
Reason for celebrity	**Q.** Why is ....? **A.** ....

6 YOUR TASK

Quiz your friends about Irish history.

Get ready to react: your friend gives a date and you give the question!

Question 1	....
Question 2	....
Question 3	....
Question 4	....
Question 5	....

Homework

Exercice 1

Complète ces questions avec *was, were* ou *did* et écris la réponse.

1. Where .... you go yesterday?

....

2. Why .... he disappear like this?

....

3. When .... you born?

....

4. When .... Bono born?

....

5. When .... the Vikings invade Ireland?

....

Exercice 2

Relis le script de la leçon p. 153.
Puis traduis les questions suivantes en anglais et réponds-y.

1. Quand est-il allé à New York ? ....

....

2. Pourquoi est-il allé à New York ? ....

....

3. Qu'a-t-il trouvé dans la grotte près de la mer ? ....

....

4. Où Rose a-t-elle rencontré Danny ? ....

....

5. Qu'est ce que Danny a donné à Rose ? ....

....

Exercice 3

Donne l'équivalent en dates des éléments suivants.

1. five days ago → ....
2. six months ago → ....
3. ten years ago → ....
4. three weeks ago → ....
5. two centuries ago → ....

Quick check

CD CLASSE → Manuel p. 117

1 **Écoute M. Fitzpatrick parler de sa vie et note ce qui s'est passé à ces dates importantes.**

- about 50 years ago: ....
- about 30 years ago: ....
- about 28 years ago: ....
- one week ago: ....
- yesterday: ....

☐ **Je sais comprendre les événements d'une vie et les resituer dans le temps.**

2 **Lis cette histoire et complète le tableau.**

In Killarney, Irish farmers were poor and they had nothing to eat. The British landlord was cruel to him so John decided to start a new life in the new world. One day, he took his bag and went to the harbour. A ship was leaving and it was going to New York. He did not know that Lucy, his future wife, was also on the boat.

Nom du héros	....
Nom de sa femme	....
Ville d'origine	....
Destination	....
Raisons du départ	....

☐ **Dans un extrait de roman, je sais comprendre l'essentiel d'une biographie.**

3 **Demande à ton ami ce qu'il a fait ce week-end. Prépare cinq questions différentes.**

1. What .... ?
2. What .... ?
3. Where .... ?
4. Who .... ?
5. When .... ?

☐ **Je sais avoir une conversation sur des événements passés de la vie quotidienne.**

Part 6

My words

Les verbes

arrive in : arriver
be born : naître
die : mourir
get engaged : se fiancer
get married : se marier
go (to): aller (à)
leave : partir
live : vivre
travel : voyager
visit : visiter

Les adjectifs

handsome : beau (pour un garçon)
pretty : mignonne (pour une fille)
lovely : adorable

Les noms

• Transport

a plane : un avion
a boat : un bateau
a bus : un bus
a coach : un autocar, un car
a ship : un navire
a train : un train

• Places

an airport : un aéroport
a harbour : un port
a train station : une gare

• Landscape

a castle : un château
a coast : une côte
a forest : une forêt
a hill : une colline
an island : une île
a lake : un lac
a landscape : un paysage
a mountain : une montagne
the sea : la mer
a town : une ville
a village : un village
a wood : un bois

• Tourism

holidays : vacances
a hotel : un hôtel
a journey : un voyage (long)
a package : un forfait tout compris
rent a car / hire a car : louer une voiture
a travel agency : une agence de voyage
a trip : un voyage (court)

Les prépositions

across : à travers (vers l'autre côté)
through : à travers (le mur)

Les expressions

Hurry up! : Dépêche toi !
It's so beautiful! : Comme c'est beau !
What a magic place! : Quel endroit magique !
Who do you think I am? : Pour qui me prends-tu ?

Maintenant je connais :

	☹	😐	☺
→ le vocabulaire du voyage	☐	☐	☐
→ les verbes pour décrire les grands événements de la vie	☐	☐	☐

Check your progress

1 LISTEN

→ Manuel p. 121

Tea time

Note ici la commande qui est faite et prépare l'addition.

Total : £.................. = ... €

J'ai su :

A1 ☐ 1. relever un ou deux éléments de la commande.

A1+ ☐ 2. relever la commande exacte.

A2 ☐ 3. comprendre pour quelle raison les clients ont fait ce choix.

....

....

2 SPEAK

→ Manuel p. 121

He lived eight centuries ago...

J'ai su :

A1 ☐ 1. donner les années de naissance et de mort dans des phrases complètes.

....

....

A1+ ☐ 2. parler de la personnalité de chaque fantôme.

....

....

3 SPEAK

→ Manuel p. 121

A musical family

J'ai su :

A1+ ☐ **1.** poser trois questions correctes sur les dates de naissance.

....

....

....

A2 ☐ **2.** poser des questions précises au passé pour obtenir plus d'informations.

....

....

4 WRITE

→ Manuel p. 121

What a horrible place!

J'ai su :

A1 ☐ **1.** exposer mon problème.

....

....

A1+ ☐ **2.** m'exclamer et dire ce que j'aimerais faire.

....

....

A2 ☐ **3.** donner des détails supplémentaires sur ma situation pour rendre mon récit plus convaincant.

....

....

Part 7 Challenges

Build up and organize your vocabulary

Challenges

FEELINGS

- angry
- ....
- ....
- ....
- ....

SPORTSMEN, SPORTSWOMEN

- a swimmer
- ....
- ....
- ....
- ....

SPORTS

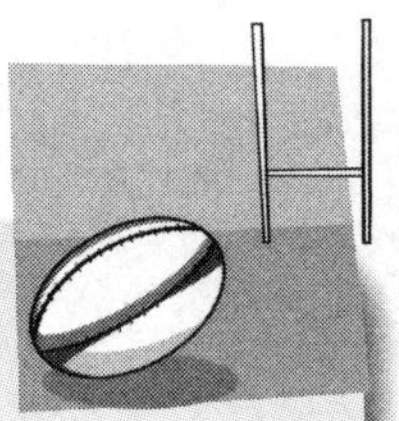

- rugby
- ....
- ....
- ....
- ....
- ....
- ....

ACTIONS IN A STADIUM

- run
- ....
- ....
- ....
- ....

A MATCH

- a team
- ....
- ....
- ....
- ....

MORE WORDS

- ....
- ....
- ....
- ....
- ....

Unit 15 Who's going to win?

Discover

→ Manuel p. 126

1 Listen and write the name of the sports. CD CLASSE

2 Read the poem in your book p. 126 and now imagine a bad day.

Today is going ....

Look at ....

....

Wordgym

a Guess who they are.

Ex.: *He plays tennis.* **You:** *He's a* ***tennis*** *player.*

He runs. He's a ....

He swims. He's a ....

He dances. He's a ....

He skis. He's a ....

He skates. He's a ....

b Qu'en déduis-tu à propos du suffixe -er ?

....

Listen and speak

CD ÉLÈVE PISTE 19 → Manuel p. 127

4 **a** **Listen to the beginning of the conversation. What are they talking about?**

....

b **Listen to Steve.**

My tactics

Steve insiste sur certains mots. Note-les.

....

• Tick the drawings which refer to Steve's personality.

☐ aggressive

☐ shy

☐ happy

☐ pretentious

• Now recap:

Steve is .... because he says ....

He is .... because he says ....

c **Listen to Tom.**

My tactics

Concentre-toi sur la voix de Tom. Note les mots sur lesquels il insiste.

....

• Concentrate on Tom's first reaction: tick the drawings which correspond to his personality.

☐ patient

☐ nervous

☐ shy

☐ happy

• Concentrate on his second reaction: tick the drawing which corresponds to his personality.

☐ nervous

☐ shy

☐ happy

☐ patient

d Listen to Tom and Steve and complete the chart with your notes.

	Steve's opinion	Tom's opinion
The match		
The players		
Their qualities		

e Listen to the end of the conversation.

• Take notes about Scarlett's opinion. ....

....

• Imagine the match result and justify your answer.

....

....

Store up your vocabulary

Note 3 nouvelles expressions que tu as apprises dans la conversation.

(Score 21 – 4): We are ....

Teddington

....

You ....!

Grammar Memo

Observe les phrases suivantes.

1. *I'm not going to run! I haven't got my trainers on!*
2. *Is he going to buy tickets for the match?*
3. *She's going to join the basketball team.*
4. *I'm playing with my friends.*

• Quelles phrases indiquent des intentions ? ....

• Quelle phrase indique une action en cours ? ....

• Que remarques-tu sur leur forme verbale ? ....

• Que peux-tu en conclure ? Pour exprimer mes intentions ou déduire ce qui va se produire, j'utilise .... conjugué au .... + ... **to** + ...

Use what you know

→ Manuel p. 128

6 Speak in pairs

Ask your friend questions about his plans for the weekend. Listen to his/her answers and complete the grid.

		Saturday		Sunday	
		Yes	No	Yes	No
 **Family**	Ex.: *Visit an old aunt*	☐	☐	☐	☐
Friends 	....	☐	☐	☐	☐
 **Hobbies**	....	☐	☐	☐	☐
TV (programmes) 	....	☐	☐	☐	☐
Others	....	☐	☐	☐	☐

7 YOUR TASK

Plan a sports camp for your class. Prepare your text! Write ideas.

MY SPORTS CAMP

Name ....

Destination ....

Accommodation (hotel, house, flat, tent…) ....

How long? .... When? ....

5 things you plan to do

- ....
- ....
- ....
- ....
- ....

5 things you are not going to do

- ....
- ....
- ....
- ....
- ....

Homework

Exercice 1

Complète les phrases. Utilise les mots ci-dessous et dis ce qui va se passer.

break rain lose win sleep

1. There are dark clouds over there.
I think it ....

2. Look at them. They are very strong rugby players!
I'm sure ....

3. Look at Chad! He's tired.
I think ....

4. Don't sit on that old chair!
I think ....

5. This team is terrible at cricket.
I'm sure ....

Exercice 2

Mr et Mrs Harrison et leurs deux enfants ont de nombreux projets pour les prochaines vacances. Écris 5 phrases sur ce qu'ils vont faire.

1. Mr Harrison: buy a car
....

2. Mrs Harrison: go swimming
....

3. Andy Harrison: learn French
....

4. Sarah Harrison: read science-fiction books
....

Exercice 3

Pose des questions sur leurs projets respectifs, et n'oublie pas la ponctuation !

1. Scarlett/visit/Tom and Chad/next year
....

2. Tom/play soccer/next month
....

3. Tom and Zoe/buy a new pet
....

4. Mrs Monroe/write/a new play
....

Quick check

Manuel p. 127

1 **Écoute et dis en français si ces personnes sont agressives, prétentieuses, polies, timides.**

1. ....
2. ....
3. ....
4. ....

☐ **Je sais identifier une personnalité grâce au ton de sa voix.**

2 **Lis cette lettre et dis si ces affirmations sont vraies ou fausses. Justifie ta réponse en français.**

Dear Tom,

I'm going to visit my uncle next weekend. He lives in London! We've got tickets for the Champions League final at Wembley stadium. I'm not going to watch this match on TV; I'm going to meet my favourite players! My uncle is going to ask for autographs and after the match, we're going to buy souvenirs. Are you going to buy tickets for the match? We could meet at Hyde Park next Saturday at 2 pm.

Write back soon.

Zack

	vrai	faux
1. La lettre a été écrite par Tom.	☐	☐
2. Zack va regarder un match à la télé.	☐	☐
3. Tom va rencontrer ses joueurs préférés.	☐	☐
4. L'oncle de Zack va demander des autographes.	☐	☐
5. Après le match ils vont visiter Hyde Park.	☐	☐

☐ **Je comprends une lettre.**

3 **Pose 4 questions à ton (ta) meilleur(e) ami(e) sur ses projets pour les prochaines vacances.**

1. .... ?
2. .... ?
3. .... ?
4. .... ?

☐ **Je sais questionner quelqu'un sur ses projets.**

Part 7

Unit 16 A champion team!

Discover

→ Manuel p. 132

Wordgym

a Listen to your teacher and write the verb below the drawing.

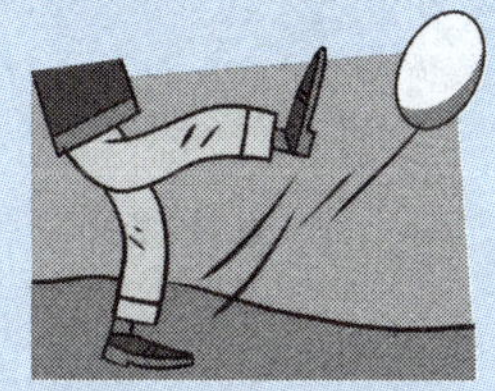

....

b Match people and actions.

supporters •	• pass the ball
players •	• gives a red card
a coach •	• cheer players on
a referee •	• trains players and gives instructions

2 Listen to the conversation. CD CLASSE

a Imagine the customer's question.

....

b Make notes in the grid.

Fortune-teller's predictions	Customer's reactions
....	....
....	....
....	....

c Do you think the customer believes the fortune-teller?

yes ☐ no ☐

....

Read and speak

→ Manuel p. 133

4 **a** **Look at the document on your book p. 133 for 15 seconds and guess what it is about.**

- **What sort of document is it?**

My tactics

Tu n'as pas lu le texte mais tu te souviens de certains éléments qui composent le document. Note-les ci-dessous.

....

....

☐ a poster ☐ an e-mail ☐ a letter ☐ a press article

- **Now recap:**

Teddington Youth news is ....

Bill Halley is ....

- **What is the document about? How do you know?**

My tactics

Faut-il lire tout le texte pour savoir de quoi il parle ? Quels éléments vont t'apporter cette information ?

....

....

It's about .... because ....

....

- **What sort of information are you going to find in the text?**

Information1: ....

Information 2: ....

b **Read the first paragraph.**

- **Why is Tom mentioned in this article?**

....

- **Find information about Tom.**

His record: ....

His qualities: ....

- **Speak about Scarlett's reaction and tick the right answers.**

☐ sorry ☐ sad ☐ impressed ☐ angry

Write words from the text to justify your answer.

....

C Read the second paragraph and take notes.

- **The final :**

Who? ....

Where? ....

When? ....

- **Why is the final important?**

....

- **Read Tom's interview and determine his personality. Tick the right answers.**

☐ scared ☐ determined ☐ disappointed ☐ confident

Write words from the text to justify your answer.

....

Store up your vocabulary

Note 2 expressions en anglais que tu as apprises dans le texte.

être confiant(e) : ....

l'esprit d'équipe : ....

Grammar Memo

Observe les phrases suivantes.

1. *He'll play at Wimbledon next June.*
2. *I won't start my training tomorrow.*
3. *Will they win the Champions'League in 2020?*

Dans les trois phrases, la forme verbale utilisée renvoie :

☐ au présent ☐ au passé ☐ au futur

Qu'en déduis-tu?

L'auxiliaire de modalité *will* permet de ....

Il est toujours accompagné de la ....

Use what you know

→ Manuel p. 134

6 Write a few lines

Imagine your life in 2025.

a Prepare your text: write ideas.

Family : ....

Job : ....

House/Flat : ....

City : ....

Means of transport : ....

Hobbies : ....

b Now write your text.

....

....

....

....

7 YOUR TASK

Play the fortune-telling game.
You're the customer. Prepare your questions and write the fortune-teller's answers.

	The customer's questions	The fortune-teller's answers	
		Yes	No
Love 	.... ? .... ?	☐	☐
 **Health**	.... ? .... ?	☐	☐
Family 	.... ? .... ?	☐	☐
 **Money**	.... ? .... ?	☐	☐
Others	.... ? .... ?	☐	☐

Homework

Exercice 1

Conjugue le verbe entre parenthèses afin de faire des prédictions.

1. Scarlett (cheer) on Tom's team next September.

....

2. I think they (lose) this match.

....

3. Tom and Chad (see) the coach tomorrow. They (be) in London with Miss Monroe.

....

4. The journalist (write) a new article tomorrow about Steve's defeat.

....

5. you (watch) the match on TV next Saturday?

....

Exercice 2

Contredis chacune de ces affirmations.

1. Manchester United will lose the match.

....

2. He won't play football tonight.

....

3. They will score 10 goals.

....

4. Scarlett won't support Tom's team.

....

5. I won't be the best rugby player.

....

Exercice 3

Remets les mots dans l'ordre pour construire une phrase.

1. ball/catch/will/Tom/the/?

....

2. will/coach/them/the/the/give/before/match/instructions

....

3. in/best/Tom/be/will/player/the/school/Teddington

....

4. his/Steve/pretentious/be/after/defeat/won't

....

Quick check

→ Manuel p. 133

1 **Lis ce document puis réponds aux questions.**

WILL ENGLAND BEAT FRANCE AT THE 6 NATIONS RUGBY?
By Terence Jenkins

Ex England Captain Lawrence Dallaglio thinks England will defeat France next year. "It will be a shock but… in my opinion, England will probably win the Six Nations", said Dallaglio.

A HOME GAME
England will play France at home at Twickenham on the last day of the tournament in February. The French team is certainly the most difficult to beat but English supporters will be there to cheer on the team.

1. Quelle est la nature de ce document ?
……………………………………
2. De quoi parle-t-il ?
……………………………………
……………………………………
3. Qui sont Terence Jenkins et Lawrence Dallaglio ? ……………………………………
……………………………………
4. Quand et où aura lieu la rencontre ?
……………………………………
5. Quel est le pronostic ? ……………………………………

☐ **Je sais comprendre globalement un extrait de journal.**

2 **Écris un e-mail à ton correspondant pour obtenir des informations sur son anniversaire (*date, party, friends, presents, cake, music*).**

From: ……………………………………
to: ……………………………………
Object: Your birthday

……………………………………
……………………………………
……………………………………

☐ **Je sais demander des renseignements sur un événement futur.**

3 **Écris un court article sur le prochain match de foot (ou un autre sport d'équipe) dans ton collège. Fais des pronostics.**

……………………………………
……………………………………
……………………………………

For more information, visit ……………………………………

☐ **Je sais écrire un court article sur un événement sportif.**

Part 7

My words

Les verbes

beat : battre
catch : attraper
cheer : acclamer
fall : tomber
hit : frapper
jump : sauter
kick : donner un coup de pied
lose : perdre
pass : passer
run : courir
score a goal : marquer un but
train : entraîner
throw : jeter, lancer
win : gagner
whistle : siffler

Les noms

cycling : le cyclisme
riding : l'équitation
a race : une course
skiing : le ski
swimming : la natation
sportsmen/sportswomen : des sportifs, des sportives
a ball : un ballon
a coach : un entraîneur
a defeat : une défaite
a fan : un supporter
a goal : un but
a game : un match
a pitch : un terrain
a referee : un arbitre
a record : un record
team spirit : l'esprit d'équipe
training : entraînement
a stadium : un stade
a team : une équipe
a training session : un entraînement
a tournament : un tournois
a victory : une victoire

Les adjectifs

bad : mauvais(e)
clumsy : maladroit(e)
confident : confiant(e)
fast : rapide
pretentious : prétentieux(euse)
shy : timide
smart : intelligent(e)
strong : fort(e)

Les expressions

hold a record : détenir un record
Teddington versus Kingston : Teddington contre Kingston
Be careful : Fais attention !
You chickens! : Poules mouillées !
Congratulations! : Félicitations !

Maintenant je connais le vocabulaire pour :

	☹	😐	☺
→ parler de différents sports	☐	☐	☐
→ parler de la personnalité de quelqu'un	☐	☐	☐
→ faire des pronostics sur un match	☐	☐	☐

Part 7 Check your progress

1 LISTEN

→ Manuel p. 137

Before the match

J'ai su :

A1 ☐ **1.** dire qui parle.

A1+ ☐ **2.** dire de quel sport ils/elles parlent.

A2 ☐ **3.** dire quelle équipe va gagner et expliquer pourquoi.

☐ **4.** dire quelle équipe va perdre et expliquer pourquoi.

2 READ

→ Manuel p. 137

A great tournament

J'ai su :

A1 ☐ **1.** dire de quel type de document il s'agit.

☐ **2.** dire de quel sport il s'agit.

A2 ☐ **3.** dire quand, où et avec qui aura lieu la rencontre.

☐ **4.** donner les atouts de chaque joueur.

3 SPEAK

Manuel p. 137

Join the team

J'ai su :

A1+

1. donner des informations sur mon identité : nom, âge, nationalité, mes capacités, mes goûts.

A2

2. expliquer mes intentions pour ce club.

4 WRITE

Manuel p. 137

My hero

J'ai su :

A1

1. présenter le joueur que je rencontrerai.

A2

2. donner des informations sur la date et le lieu de notre rencontre.

3. imaginer ce qu'il/elle fera lors de cette rencontre.

4. imaginer ce que je ferai ou ne ferai pas.

# ÉCOUTER	Je note avec mon professeur les activités du manuel et du workbook qui correspondent :
Part 1	
• Repérer le lexique de l'école et de l'identité de quelqu'un.	....
• Repérer le lexique des ordres et demandes.	....
• Repérer qui parle.	....
• Repérer des sentiments.	....
Part 2	
• Comprendre des informations sur une maison.	....
• Repérer le lexique de la maison.	....
• Comprendre ce qu'une personne aime ou n'aime pas.	....
Part 3	
• Comprendre où se situent précisément les choses.	....
• Comprendre un itinéraire.	....
• Repérer le lexique lié à la visite des monuments.	....
Part 4	
• Repérer le lexique de la famille	....
• Comprendre des informations sur les goûts, les activités et le quotidien de quelqu'un.	....
• Comprendre à qui appartient un objet.	....
• Comprendre le récit d'une excursion.	....
• Repérer le lexique de la ville.	....
Part 5	
• Comprendre les arguments d'un candidat pendant une audition.	....
• Repérer des émotions et des sentiments.	....
• Comprendre ce qui est en train de se passer.	....
• Comprendre ce que quelqu'un a dû faire.	....
• Comprendre une interview.	....
Part 6	
• Comprendre des informations sur un voyage.	....
• Repérer le lexique du voyage et des transports.	....
• Comprendre des éléments de chronologie.	....
Part 7	
• Comprendre des prédictions.	....
• Repérer le lexique du sport.	....
• Comprendre les intentions de quelqu'un.	....

Je peux comprendre des mots familiers et des expressions très courantes au sujet de moi-même, de ma famille et de l'environnement concret et immédiat, si les gens parlent lentement et distinctement. A1 / A1+ ☹	☹ / ☺ (neutre) 😐	☺	Pour m'améliorer, je relis et je retravaille :
☐	☐	☐	• Discover 1 p. 18 ; Practice your vocabulary p. 22 ; English Lab p. 21
☐	☐	☐	• Practice your pronunciation p. 22 ; Discover 2 p. 18
☐	☐	☐	• Tactics p. 25 ; English Lab p. 27
☐	☐	☐	• Tactics p.19 ; Discover 3 p.18
☐	☐	☐	• Discover 1 p. 34 ; Wordgym WB p. 27
☐	☐	☐	• Discover 1 p. 40 ; Practice your vocabulary p. 44 ; Wordgym WB p. 33
☐	☐	☐	• Discover 2 p. 40 ; Tactics p. 35 ; Discover 3 p. 34
☐	☐	☐	• Discover 1 p. 50 ; Prépositions p. 34 et p. 50
☐	☐	☐	• Discover 2 p. 50 ; English Lab p. 53 ; Discover 1b p. 56
☐	☐	☐	• Wordgym WB p. 49 ; Quick check WB p. 54
☐	☐	☐	• Discover 2 p. 66 ; Chanson « Vampire Song » p. 68
☐	☐	☐	• Discover 2 p. 72
☐	☐	☐	• Discover 2 p. 78
☐	☐	☐	• Discover 1 p. 66
☐	☐	☐	• Discover 1 p. 78
☐	☐	☐	• Discover 1 et 2 p. 88
☐	☐	☐	• Listen and speak p. 89
☐	☐	☐	• Listen and speak p. 89
☐	☐	☐	• Quick check WB p. 86
☐	☐	☐	• Discover 2 p. 88
☐	☐	☐	• Discover 2 p. 110
☐	☐	☐	• Listen and speak p. 111
☐	☐	☐	• Discover 3 p. 116
☐	☐	☐	• Discover 1 p. 126
☐	☐	☐	• Tactics p. 127 ; Discover 2 p. 132 ; Quick check 1 WB p. 124
☐	☐	☐	• Grammar p. 135 ; Discover 1 p. 132 ; Wordgym p. 125

LIRE	Je note avec mon professeur les activités du manuel et du workbook qui correspondent :
Part 1 • Comprendre un e-mail. • Comprendre les consignes.	....
Part 2 • Comprendre une description dans une carte postale. • Comprendre un court poème sur les goûts de quelqu'un.	....
Part 3 • Comprendre les informations essentielles d'une brochure touristique. • Comprendre des recommandations. Comprendre les règles à respecter lors de la visite d'un monument.	....
Part 4 • Comprendre un emploi du temps. • Comprendre un « chant » au sujet de la nourriture. • Comprendre un message racontant les événements d'un week-end.	....
Part 5 • Identifier les personnages dans un récit. • Répondre à un questionnaire sur les styles vestimentaires. • Comprendre l'essentiel de la critique d'un spectacle.	....
Part 6 • Comprendre une légende. • Comprendre une frise chronologique.	....
Part 7 • Comprendre un court poème. • Comprendre l'essentiel d'un court article de presse.	....

Je peux comprendre des noms familiers, des mots, ainsi que des phrases très simples, par exemple dans des annonces, des affiches ou des catalogues. Je peux également comprendre le sens général de documents écrits courants, simples et très courts en repérant des noms et mots familiers sans pour autant comprendre tout le texte. A1 / A1+ ☹ 😐 ☺	Pour m'améliorer, je relis et je retravaille :
☐ ☐ ☐	• Write a few lines p. 20
☐ ☐ ☐	• Discover 1 p. 24
☐ ☐ ☐	• My words p. 35 ; WB p. 33
☐ ☐ ☐	• Wordgym p. 35 ; WB p. 27 ; My Words p. 40 ; WB p. 39 ; Discover 1 et 2 p. 40
☐ ☐ ☐	• My Words WB p. 43 ; Grammar : There is/There are p. 53 ; Tactics p. 51
☐ ☐ ☐	• Ex 3. p. 60 ; Speak for a minute p. 58 ; Grammar Must/Mustn't p. 59
☐ ☐ ☐	• Discover 2 p. 66 ; Language practice 3 p. 70
☐ ☐ ☐	• My words WB p. 77
☐ ☐ ☐	• Les verbes p. 79 ; Grammar : Le prétérit p. 81
☐ ☐ ☐	• Tactics, Read and speak p. 101
☐ ☐ ☐	• Ex 1 et 2 p. 98
☐ ☐ ☐	• Ex 2 et 3 p. 104
☐ ☐ ☐	• Discover 2 p. 116 ; Wordgym WB p. 109
☐ ☐ ☐	• Words to remember p. 117 ; Grammar p. 119
☐ ☐ ☐	• Discover 2 p. 126 ; Discover 3 p. 132 ; Tactics p. 133
☐ ☐ ☐	• Read and speak p. 133

	PARLER EN CONTINU	Je note avec mon professeur les activités du manuel et du workbook qui correspondent :
Part 1	• Présenter un ou une ami(e). • Donner des ordres et demander quelque chose poliment.	....
Part 2	• Présenter la maison de quelqu'un. Décrire une pièce de la maison. • Présenter un personnage et parler de ses goûts.	....
Part 3	• Décrire un lieu, dire ce que l'on y trouve. • Indiquer un itinéraire à quelqu'un. • Donner les règles à suivre lors de la visite d'un monument.	....
Part 4	• Présenter l'emploi du temps de quelqu'un, ses activités et ses habitudes. • Dire à qui appartient telle ou telle chose. • Présenter ce que quelqu'un a fait lors d'une excursion.	....
Part 5	• Comparer deux personnes entre elles. • Décrire une action en cours, un problème. • Décrire un problème et dire ce que l'on a dû faire.	....
Part 6	• Parler des projets de quelqu'un. • Raconter des événements passés. • Situer des événements dans le passé.	....
Part 7	• Parler de mes projets pour des vacances. • Faire des promesses pour obtenir quelque chose.	....

Je peux utiliser des expressions et des phrases simples pour décrire mon lieu d'habitation, ma famille et d'autres personnes ainsi que mon environnement concret et immédiat. A1 / A1+			Pour m'améliorer, je relis et je retravaille :
☹	😐	☺	
☐	☐	☐	• Discover 2 p. 18 ; Ex 2 WB p. 15
☐	☐	☐	• Grammar p. 27
☐	☐	☐	• English Lab p. 37 ; My words WB p. 39 ; Grammar p. 37
☐	☐	☐	• Discover 1 et 2 p. 40 ; Words to remember p. 41 ; Grammar : I like/I don't like
☐	☐	☐	• Les prépositions p. 34 et p. 50 ; Discover 1 p. 50 ; Ex 1 p. 53 ; Speak for a minute p. 52
☐	☐	☐	• My words WB p. 55 ; Ex 4. p. 60 ; Discover 2 p. 56
☐	☐	☐	• Ex 1 p. 59 ; Speak for a minute p. 58 ; My words WB p. 55 ; Homework WB p. 52
☐	☐	☐	• Ex 1, 2, 3 p. 69 ; Speak for a minute p. 68 ; Discover 2 p. 66
☐	☐	☐	• Discover 2 p. 72 ; Speak for a minute p. 74 ; Grammar p. 75 ; Ex. 1 p. 75
☐	☐	☐	• Discover 2 p. 78 ; Speak for a minute p. 80 ; Grammar p. 81 ; Ex 1, 2, 3 p. 81
☐	☐	☐	• Discover 2 p. 88 ; Grammar p. 91
☐	☐	☐	• Listen and speak p. 95 ; Grammar p. 97
☐	☐	☐	• Discover 2 p. 100 ; Grammar p. 103
☐	☐	☐	• Discover 2 p. 110 ; Ex 1 p. 113 ;
☐	☐	☐	• Speak in pairs p. 118 ;
☐	☐	☐	• Ex 3 p. 119
☐	☐	☐	• Grammar p. 129
☐	☐	☐	• Use what you know 5 et 6 p. 128

# PARLER EN INTERACTION		Je note avec mon professeur les activités du manuel et du workbook qui correspondent :
Part 1	• Me renseigner sur l'identité de quelqu'un.	....
	• Faire un quiz sur l'histoire et la géographie.	....
Part 2	• Me renseigner sur ce que quelqu'un possède.	....
	• Interroger mes camarades sur leur identité et sur leurs goûts.	....
Part 3	• Me renseigner sur ce que l'on trouve dans un lieu particulier.	....
	• Acheter des souvenirs.	....
	• Me renseigner sur ce que quelqu'un est capable de faire.	....
	• Me renseigner sur un itinéraire.	....
Part 4	• Me renseigner sur la vie quotidienne, les activités et les goûts de quelqu'un.	....
	• Me renseigner sur l'appartenance de tel ou tel objet.	....
	• Me renseigner sur ce que quelqu'un a fait pendant le week-end.	....
Part 5	• Choisir un candidat et justifier mon choix.	....
	• Parler de ce qui est en train de se passer.	....
	• Interviewer quelqu'un sur ses expériences.	....
Part 6	• Poser des questions sur des célébrités irlandaises et y répondre.	....
	• Partager mes sentiments et mes réactions.	....
	• Discuter de ce que l'on aimerait faire.	....
Part 7	• Discuter du programme d'un week-end.	....
	• Interroger une voyante.	....

Je peux communiquer, de façon simple, à condition que l'interlocuteur soit disposé à répéter ou à reformuler ses phrases plus ntement et à m'aider à formuler ce que j'essaie de dire. Je peux poser des questions simples et y répondre si l'échange est bref. A1 / A1+			Pour m'améliorer, je relis et je retravaille :
☹	😐	☺	
☐	☐	☐	• Grammar : Les questions p. 21 ; Ex 3 p. 22
☐	☐	☐	• Speak in pairs p. 26
☐	☐	☐	• Grammar p. 37 ; Ex 2 p. 37 ; Ex p. 154 ; Speak in pairs p. 36
☐	☐	☐	• Speak in pairs p. 42 ; Wordgym WB p. 33 ; Ex 5 p. 44
☐	☐	☐	• Grammar p. 53 ; Your Task p. 52
☐	☐	☐	• Grammar Is/are there? ; Ex 2 p. 53
☐	☐	☐	• Grammar Can/can't p. 59 ; Speak in pairs p. 58
☐	☐	☐	• Discover 1 p. 56 ; Your task p. 58
☐	☐	☐	• Discover 2c p. 66 ; Your task p. 68
☐	☐	☐	• Ex 1, 2, 3 p. 69 ; Ex 3 p. 70
☐	☐	☐	• Ex 2, 3 p. 75 ; Speak in pairs p. 74
☐	☐	☐	• Use what you know p. 96
☐	☐	☐	• Ex 1, 2 et 3 p. 97
☐	☐	☐	• Discover 2 p. 100
☐	☐	☐	• Speak in pairs p. 118
☐	☐	☐	• Listen and speak p. 117
☐	☐	☐	• Discover 2 et 3 p. 110
☐	☐	☐	• Grammar p. 135
☐	☐	☐	• Discover 2 p. 132

	# ÉCRIRE	Je note avec mon professeur les activités du manuel et du workbook qui correspondent :
Part 1	• Présenter son école et ses professeurs. • Préparer des questions pour un quiz.	....
Part 2	• Imaginer la chambre d'une célébrité. • Écrire un poème sur mes goûts.	....
Part 3	• Raconter brièvement une visite touristique. • Écrire le programme de la visite d'un château.	....
Part 4	• Préparer des questions pour un sondage et décrire le quotidien, les goûts et les activités de quelqu'un. • Écrire un e-mail pour raconter ce que l'on a fait lors d'une visite à Londres.	....
Part 5	• Décrire ses qualités pour un rôle. • Raconter le déroulement d'une « première ». • Réécrire un court article.	....
Part 6	• Écrire un e-mail à l'Office de tourisme d'Irlande pour demander des renseignement. • Compléter un axe du temps.	....
Part 7	• Écrire le programme d'un séjour en camp de sport. • Imaginer sa vie en 2025 et la raconter.	....

Je peux écrire des notes et messages simples et très courts s'il s'agit de sujets familiers et concernant mon environnement immédiat (carte postale). Je peux compléter un questionnaire simple(inscrire par exemple mon nom, ma nationalité et mon adresse sur une fiche de renseignements). A1 / A1+			Pour m'améliorer, je relis et je retravaille :
☹	😐	☺	
☐	☐	☐	• Discover 1 p. 18 ; Ex 3 p. 21
☐	☐	☐	• Ex p.154
☐	☐	☐	• Prépositions p. 34 ; Lexique WB p. 39 ; Speak for a minute p. 36 ; Ex 3 WB p. 31
☐	☐	☐	• Ex 1 p. 40 ; My words WB p. 39
☐	☐	☐	• Grammar Must/mustn't p. 59
☐	☐	☐	• Brochure p. 51 ; My words WB p. 55
☐	☐	☐	• Ex 3 p. 70 ; My words WB p. 77 ; Read and speak p. 79
☐	☐	☐	• Your task p. 80 ; Grammar : Le prétérit p. 81 ; Ex 2 p. 8
☐	☐	☐	• Words to remember p. 89 ; Grammar : le comparatif p. 91
☐	☐	☐	• Speak for a minute p. 103 ; Grammar p. 97
☐	☐	☐	• Grammar p. 103
☐	☐	☐	• Listen and speak p. 117
☐	☐	☐	• Discover 3 p. 116
☐	☐	☐	• Grammar p.129 ; Language practice p. 130
☐	☐	☐	• Grammar p.135 ; Language practice p. 136

Crédits photographiques

Couverture

hg :	Orédia/Sébastien Godere
hd :	Shutterstock/Ken McDougall
b :	Getty/Image Bank/Geoffrey Clifford
20h :	Getty/Travelpix Ltd
20bg :	Rapho/Xavier Desmier
20bd :	Age/Alan Copson
48 :	Shutterstock/WH Chow
98g :	Gamma/UPI/Rune Hellestad
98d :	Sipa/AP/Kevork Djansezian

N° d'éditeur : 10187581 - Depôt légal - juin 2012
Imprimé en Italie par Grafica Veneta SpA